D0460164

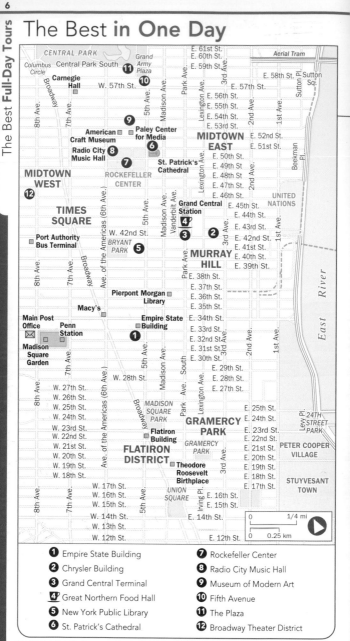

The Best **in One Day**

- **1** Empire State Building
- **2** Chrysler Building
- **3** Grand Central Terminal
- **4** Great Northern Food Hall
- **5** New York Public Library
- **6** St. Patrick's Cathedral
- **7** Rockefeller Center
- **8** Radio City Music Hall
- **9** Museum of Modern Art
- **10** Fifth Avenue
- **11** The Plaza
- **12** Broadway Theater District

Previous page: Gazing over Manhattan from the Top of the Rock viewing platform.

The most wonderful—and maddening—thing about New York? The endless number of choices. Start your urban exploration in Midtown, the city's business and commercial heart. The shopping opportunities here are legion, and the air space is spiky with corporate skyscrapers—but Midtown is also home to several quintessential New York landmarks. START: **Subway 6 to 33rd Street or B, D, F, M, N, Q, or R to 34th Street.**

❶ ★★ Empire State Building.
King Kong climbed it in 1933. A plane slammed into it in 1945. After September 11, 2001, the Empire State regained its status as New York City's tallest building . . . at least for a few years. Through it all, it has remained one of the city's favorite landmarks. Completed in 1931, the limestone-and-stainless-steel Art Deco dazzler climbs 103 stories (1,454 ft./436m). The best views are from the 86th- and 102nd-floor observatories, but I prefer the former for its windswept deck (upstairs you stay inside). From up here, the citywide panorama is electric. Lines can be long. ⏱ *2 hr. 350 Fifth Ave. (at 34th St.). www. esbnyc.com.* ☎ *212/736-3100. Observatory admission (86th floor) $25 adults, $22 seniors, $19 children 6–12, free for children 5 and under. ESB Express pass: $48. 102nd floor observatory: $15 extra. Observatories open daily 8am–2am; last elevator goes up at 1:15am. Subway: 6 to 33rd St., B/D/F/M to 34th St.*

❷ ★★★ Chrysler Building
Built as the Chrysler Corporation headquarters in 1930, this is New York's most romantic Art Deco edifice and, for many New Yorkers, its most endearing visual touchstone. It's especially dramatic at night, when the triangular points in its steely crown are outlined in silvery lights. Go in to see the marble-clad lobby; a mural on the ceiling was actually rediscovered in 1999. Alas,

you can't go beyond the lobby. *See p 34.*

❸ ★★ Grand Central Terminal.
An iconic Beaux Arts beauty. The highlight is the vast, imposing main concourse, where high windows allow sunlight to pour onto the half-acre (.25-hectare) Tennessee-marble floor. Everything gleams, from the brass clock over the central kiosk to the gold- and nickel-plated chandeliers piercing the side archways. The breathtaking *Sky Ceiling* depicts the constellations of the winter sky above New York. *42nd St. and Park Ave. www.grand centralterminal.com.* ☎ *212/340-2210. Subway: 4/5/6/7/S to 42nd St.*

Gargoyles perched high on the Chrysler Building.

4️⃣ ★ Great Northern Food Hall. You're at Grand Central already, so stay here to nosh on Nordic fare—everything from open sandwiches to fancy porridge—at this upscale food court, created by Claus Meyer, co-founder of Noma in Copenhagen (considered by many the world's best restaurant). Downstairs is the famous Oyster Bar, another excellent choice. $–$$.

5️⃣ ★ New York Public Library. The lions *Patience* and *Fortitude* stand guard outside the grand Fifth Avenue entrance of the **Main Branch (Stephen A. Schwarzman Building)** of the public library, designed by Carrère & Hastings in 1911. It's one of the country's finest examples of Beaux Arts architecture. Sadly, architect John Mervin Carrère never got to enjoy the fruits of his labor; he was killed in a taxi accident 2 months before the library dedication. The majestic white-marble structure is clad with Corinthian columns and allegorical statues. The original Winnie the Pooh stuffed bear is on display in the library's Children's Center. ⏱ *1 hr. Fifth Ave. (btw. 42nd and 40th sts.). www. nypl.org.* ☎ *917/275-6975. Free admission. Mon and Thurs–Sat 10am–6pm, Tues–Wed 10am–8pm, Sun 1–5pm. Subway: B/D/F/M to 42nd St.*

6️⃣ ★★ St. Patrick's Cathedral. This Neo-Gothic white-marble-and-stone wonder is the largest Roman Catholic cathedral in the U.S. Designed by James Renwick, begun in 1859, and consecrated in 1879, St. Patrick's wasn't completed until 1906. You can pop in between services to get a look at the impressive interior. The St. Michael and St. Louis altar came from Tiffany & Co., while the St. Elizabeth altar—honoring Mother Elizabeth Ann Seton, the first American-born

saint—was designed by Paolo Medici of Rome. ⏱ *15 min. Fifth Ave. (btw. 50th and 51st sts.). www.saintpatricks cathedral.org.* ☎ *212/753-2261. Free admission. Daily 6:30am–8:45pm. Subway: B/D/F/M to 47th–50th sts./Rockefeller Center.*

7️⃣ ★★★ Rockefeller Center. A prime example of civic optimism expressed in soaring architecture, Rock Center was built in the 1930s at the height of the Great Depression. It's now the world's largest privately owned business-and-entertainment center, with 18 buildings on 21 acres. The **GE Building,** also known as **30 Rock,** at 30 Rockefeller Plaza, is a 70-story showpiece; at its apex is the **Top of the Rock** observation deck. In season the mammoth Rockefeller Center Christmas tree towers over the 30 Rock plaza and its famous skating rink. *Bounded by 48th and 51st sts. and Fifth and Sixth aves. Timed tickets to Top of the Rock $26–$32 (www.topoftherock nyc.com). Subway: B/D/F/M to 47th–50th sts./Rockefeller Center.*

The Sky Ceiling at Grand Central Terminal.

Inside St. Patrick's Cathedral on Fifth Avenue.

8 ★★★ Radio City Music Hall. Opened in 1932, this sumptuous Art Deco classic is the world's largest indoor theater, with 6,000 seats. Long known for its Rockettes revues and popular Christmas show, Radio City also has a place in movie history: More than 700 films have opened here since 1933. The Deco "powder rooms" are some of the swankiest in town. *1260 Sixth Ave. (at 50th St.). www.radiocity.com.* ☎ *212/247-4777. 1-hr. Stage Door Tour daily 11am–3pm (extended hours Nov 15–Dec 30). Tickets $23 adults, $18 seniors, $16 children 12 and under. Subway: B/D/F/M to 47th–50th sts./Rockefeller Center.*

9 ★★★ Museum of Modern Art. MoMA houses the world's greatest collection of painting and sculpture from the late 19th century and 20th century—from Monet's Water Lilies and Klimt's The Kiss to 20th-century masterworks by Frida Kahlo and Jasper Johns to contemporary pieces by Richard Serra and Chuck Close. Add to that a vast collection of modern drawings, photos, architectural models and modern furniture, iconic design objects ranging from tableware to sports cars, and film and video. ① *3 hr. See p 52.*

10 ★★ Fifth Avenue. New York's most famous shopping artery runs up to the southeast corner of Central Park at 59th Street. Some landmarks to note: **Henri Bendel,** at no. 712 (btw. 55th and 56th sts.), a whimsical department store with vintage Lalique art-glass windows; **Tiffany & Co.,** at no. 727 (btw. 56th and 57th sts.), with its stainless-steel doors and Atlas clock; and the shop that clothes the 1%: **Bergdorf Goodman** at 754 (at 57th St.). *Subway: N/R/W to Fifth Ave./59th St.*

11 ★ The Plaza. There's no denying the glamour of the Big Apple's most famous hotel (now divided between hotel rooms and private condos, with restaurants and shops on the lowest floors). This 1907 French Renaissance "palace" has hosted royalty, celebrities, and a legion of honeymooners. Have afternoon tea in the legendary **Palm Court** or sip a flute of bubbly in the **Champagne Bar.** *768 Fifth Ave. (at Central Park South) www.fairmont.com/theplaza.* ☎ *800/850-0909. Subway: N/R/W to Fifth Ave./59th St.*

12 ★★★ "Broadway Theater District." You can't say you've "done" NYC until you've experienced a big, splashy musical or thought-provoking drama. See p 149 for tips on how to save money on tickets.

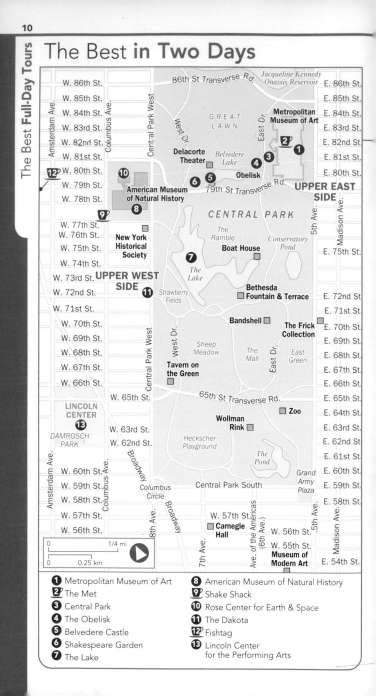

The Best **in Two Days**

1 Metropolitan Museum of Art
2 The Met
3 Central Park
4 The Obelisk
5 Belvedere Castle
6 Shakespeare Garden
7 The Lake
8 American Museum of Natural History
9 Shake Shack
10 Rose Center for Earth & Space
11 The Dakota
12 Fishtag
13 Lincoln Center for the Performing Arts

After the 1-day tour of Midtown, head uptown to Manhattan's artistic soul—the Metropolitan Museum and Lincoln Center. The area is also home to Central Park, an urban oasis that recharges body and mind. This part of town has a wealth of museums—most of them along Fifth Avenue. To avoid burnout, don't try to see them all in 1 day. If you have kids in tow, run, don't walk, to the American Museum of Natural History. START: **Subway 4, 5, or 6 to 86th Street.**

❶ ★★★ Metropolitan Museum of Art. At 1.6 million sq. ft. (148,644 sq. m), this is the largest museum in the Western Hemisphere, attracting five million visitors annually. Nearly all the world's cultures through the ages are on display—from Egyptian mummies to ancient Greek statuary to Islamic carvings to Renaissance paintings to 20th-century decorative arts—and masterpieces are the rule. You could go once a week for a lifetime and still find something new on each visit. Everyone should see the **Temple of Dendur,** the jewel of the Egyptian collection. But let personal preference be your guide to the rest. Touchstones include the exceptional Rembrandts, Vermeers, and other Dutch master painters. Transplanted period rooms—from the elegant 18th-century bedroom from a Venetian castle to the warm

and inviting 20th-century Frank Lloyd Wright living room—are equally unmissable. ⏱ *3 hr. See p 42.*

❷ The Met. Eating at the Met gives you options. If you're visiting between May and October, check out the Roof Garden Bar ($) for breathtaking treetop views of Central Park. Year-round you can grab lunch at the ground-floor cafeteria ($), the American Art Café ($$), or the elegant Petrie Court Café ($$) with its own park vistas. On Friday and Saturday evenings, cocktails and appetizers are served at the Great Hall Balcony Bar ($) overlooking the Great Hall. *Fifth Ave. (at 82nd St.). www.metmuseum.org.* ☎ *212/535-7710.*

❸ ★★★ kids Central Park. Manhattanites may lack yards, but

The Metropolitan Museum of Art's American Wing.

they do have this glorious swath of green. Designed by Frederick Law Olmstead and Calvert Vaux in the 1850s, the park is 2½ miles (4km) long (extending from 59th to 110th sts.) and a half-mile (.8km) wide (from Fifth Ave. to Central Park West). It encompasses a zoo, a carousel, two ice-skating rinks (in season), restaurants, children's playgrounds, and even theaters. *See p 100.*

❹ **The Obelisk.** Also called Cleopatra's Needle, this 71-ft. (21m) obelisk is reached by following the path leading west behind the Met. Originally erected in Heliopolis, Egypt, around 1475 B.C., it was given to New York by the khedive of Egypt in 1880. Continue on the path to Central Park's **Great Lawn** (p 101), site of countless softball games, concerts, and peaceful political protests.

❺ ★ **Belvedere Castle.** Built by Calvert Vaux in 1869, this fanciful medieval-style fortress-in-miniature sits at the highest point in Central Park and affords sweeping views. The many birds that call this area home led to the creation of a bird-watching and educational center in the castle's ranger station. To get here, follow the path across East Drive and walk west.

❻ **Shakespeare Garden.** Next to the Delacorte Theater, this garden grows flowers and plants mentioned in the Bard's plays.

❼ ★★ **The Lake.** South of the garden, you'll reach the Lake, with its iconic photo-op outlooks at **Bow Bridge** and **Bethesda Terrace.** Follow the perimeter pathway lined with weeping willows and Japanese cherry trees east to the neo-Victorian **Loeb Boathouse,** which rents rowboats and bicycles; on summer evenings, you can arrange gondola rides. Returning to the west side, follow paths to exit the park at 77th Street and Central Park West. *See p 102.*

❽ ★★★ 𝐤𝐢𝐝𝐬 **American Museum of Natural History.** The spectacular entrance—featuring a ***Barosaurus*** skeleton, the world's largest freestanding dinosaur exhibit—is just the tip of the iceberg. Founded in 1869, the AMNH houses the world's greatest natural-science collection in a square-block group of buildings made of whimsical towers and turrets, pink granite, and red brick. The diversity of the holdings is astounding: some 36 million specimens, ranging from microscopic organisms to the world's largest cut gem, the **Brazilian Princess Topaz** (21,005 carats). If you only see one exhibit, make it the ★ dinosaurs,

The T. Rex at the American Museum of Natural History.

which take up the entire fourth floor. *Note:* The admission lines can be tedious for young kids. If you buy advance tickets online, you can avoid the 20-minute wait. ① *2 hr. See p 50.*

9 **kids** **Shake Shack.** The food offerings at the AMNH are less impressive than the artifacts. Instead of dining here, duck across the street (west of the museum) to this New York–founded chain for excellent burgers, fries and creamy shakes. *366 Columbus Ave (at W. 77th St. www.shakeshack.com.* ☎ *646/747-8770. $.*

Central Park photo-op: The Imagine mosaic at Strawberry Fields.

10 ★★ **kids** **Rose Center for Earth & Space.** Part of the American Museum of Natural History, this four-story sphere "floating" in a glass square is astonishing. Even if you're suffering from museum overload, the Rose Center will lift your spirits. The center's **Hayden Planetarium** features spectacular space shows (every half-hour Mon–Fri 10:30am–4:30pm, Wed from 11am; Sat–Sun 10:30am–5pm). *See p 51.*

11 **The Dakota and Strawberry Fields.** The 1884 apartment house with dark trim and dramatic gables, dormers, and oriel windows is best known as the spot where its most famous resident, John Lennon, was gunned down on December 8, 1980 (Yoko Ono still lives here). Directly across the street from the Dakota in Central Park is **Strawberry Fields,** a memorial to the songwriter and peace activist. A must for serious Beatles fans. *1 W. 72nd St. (at Central Park West) and Central Park btw. 71st and 74th sts.*

12 **Fishtag.** As the name suggests, the fruits of the sea are celebrated at this buzzy, sometimes loud, townhouse restaurant. That includes many types of fish cured or smoked in house; Greek-style preparations which might feature a fresh catch simply grilled with lemon and olive oil; and more creative dishes, like my sinful favorite: branzino stuffed with head cheese. *222 W. 79th St. (btw. Broadway and Amsterdam Ave.). http://michaelpsilakis com/fishtag.* ☎ *212/362-7470. $$.*

13 ★★ **Lincoln Center for the Performing Arts.** New York has countless performing arts venues, but none so multifaceted as Lincoln Center—presenting world-class opera, ballet, theater, jazz, symphonies, and more. After a long day on your feet, relax on the outdoor plaza in front of the fountains or on the tilting roof lawn. At Christmas time, the light displays are lovely, and on summer evenings, the plaza becomes an outdoor dance party. *See p 145.*

The Best in Three Days

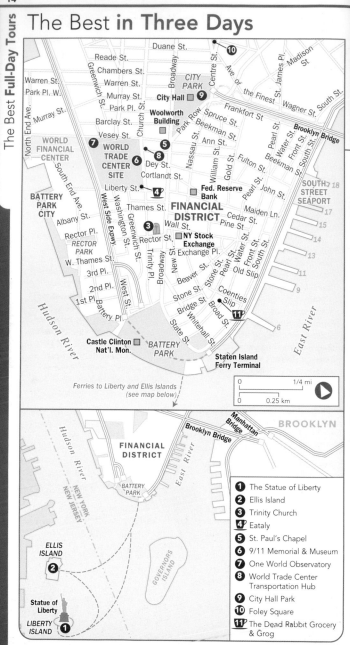

Reade St.
Duane St.
Chambers St.
Warren St.
Murray St.
Park Pl.
Barclay St.
Vesey St.

Warren St.
Park Pl. W.
Murray St.

North End Ave.

Greenwich St.

Broadway

CITY
HALL
PARK

City Hall

Church St.

Woolworth
Building

WORLD
FINANCIAL
CENTER

WORLD
TRADE
CENTER
SITE

Park Row

Spruce St.

Centre St.

Ave. of
the Finest

Frankfort St

Beekman St.
Ann St.

Nassau St.

William St.

Madison
St

James Pl.

Wagner Pl.

South St.

Brooklyn Bridge

Pearl St.

Water St.

Front St.

Fulton St.

Beekman St.

South St.

BATTERY
PARK
CITY

South End Ave.

Dey St.

Cortlandt St.

Liberty St.

Albany St.

Rector Pl.

RECTOR
PARK

W. Thames St.

3rd Pl.

2nd Pl.

1st Pl

West Side Expwy.

Washington St.

Greenwich St.

Thames St.

Fed. Reserve
Bank

Gold St.

FINANCIAL
DISTRICT

Wall St.

Rector St.

Trinity Pl.

Broadway

New St.

Beaver St.

Stone St.

Bridge St.

Whitehall St.

Broad St.

NY Stock
Exchange

Exchange Pl.

Pine St.

Maiden Ln.

Cedar St.

John St.

Pearl St.

Water St.

Front St.

South St.

Old Slip

Coenties
Slip

SOUTH
STREET
SEAPORT

18

17

15

14

13

11

9

6

West St.

Battery Pl.

State St.

Castle Clinton
Nat'l. Mon.

BATTERY
PARK

Staten Island
Ferry Terminal

Hudson River

East River

Ferries to Liberty and Ellis Islands
(see map below)

0   1/4 mi

0   0.25 km

Hudson River

Manhattan
Bridge

BROOKLYN

FINANCIAL
DISTRICT

Brooklyn Bridge

East River

NEW YORK
NEW JERSEY

BATTERY
PARK

GOVERNORS
ISLAND

ELLIS
ISLAND

Statue of
Liberty

LIBERTY
ISLAND

❶ The Statue of Liberty
❷ Ellis Island
❸ Trinity Church
❹ Eataly
❺ St. Paul's Chapel
❻ 9/11 Memorial & Museum
❼ One World Observatory
❽ World Trade Center
   Transportation Hub
❾ City Hall Park
❿ Foley Square
⓫ The Dead Rabbit Grocery
   & Grog

Explore the city's beginnings, its turbulent recent history, and its dynamic present in Lower Manhattan. You'll find colonial influences and cobblestoned streets, a center of city government and world finance, the Statue of Liberty and Ellis Island, and a neighborhood that still bears the scars of the September 11, 2001, terrorist attacks. (Don't miss the museum and memorial at the World Trade Center site.) We recommend that you start this tour early, and book visits to both the 9/11 Museum and Lady Liberty well in advance. For more details on southern Manhattan, see p 56. START: Subway 4, 5, or 6 to Brooklyn Bridge/City Hall.

❶ ★★★ kids The Statue of Liberty. For the millions who arrived in New York by ship, Lady Liberty was their first glimpse of America. A gift from France to the U.S., the statue was designed by sculptor Frédéric-Auguste Bartholdi and unveiled on October 28, 1886. Seeing her is as much of a thrill today as it was then. *Note:* Save yourself a potentially 3-hour wait by buying and printing tickets ahead of time and getting to the ferry at least half an hour before it starts operating. Standard tickets sell out daily by noon, but you'll need to book as much as 3 months in advance for tickets to go up to the crown (you'll climb 377 un-air-conditioned steps, but the view, and the sight of Gustave Eiffel's handsome interior scaffolding –yes, THAT Eiffel—is worth it). Only advance tickets include access to the Statue of Liberty Museum and the pedestal's observation deck. *Tip:* While only official Statue Cruises dock at Liberty Island, a free 25-minute ride on the Staten Island Ferry (www.siferry.com) also provides spectacular skyline views of Manhattan and is a wonderful way to see the harbor. ⏱ *1 hr. (Statue Cruise ferry also visits Ellis Island, see below.) Liberty Island. www.nps.gov/stli and www.statuecruises.com. ☎ 212/363-3200 (general info) or 877/523-9849 (tickets). Tickets $18 adults, $14 seniors, $9 children 4–12; crown access $21 adults, $17 seniors, $12 children. Daily 9am–4pm (last ferry departs around 3pm); extended hours in summer. Subway: 4/5 to Bowling Green; 1/9 to South Ferry.*

❷ ★★★ Ellis Island Immigration Museum. For 62 years

Piles of immigrants' luggage on display at the Ellis Island Museum.

(1892–1954), this was the main point of entry for newcomers to America. Today it's one of New York's most moving attractions—particularly for the 40% of Americans whose ancestors first set foot in "The New World" here. The self-guided tour follows the path immigrants would have taken (as they underwent health exams, a grilling on their political beliefs, and more) before learning whether or not they'd be admitted into the country. Recently, the un-renovated hospital building has opened for an extra-cost, but fascinating, "hard hat" tour (see website for details). ⏱ *2 hr. Ellis Island. www.nps.gov/elis. For tickets and ferry info see Statue of Liberty, above. Daily 9:30am–5pm; extended hours in summer. Subway: 4/5 to Bowling Green; 1/9 to South Ferry.*

❸ ★★ **Trinity Church.** This neo-Gothic marvel was consecrated in 1846 and is still active today. The main doors, modeled on the doors in Florence's Baptistry, are decorated with biblical scenes; inside are splendid stained-glass windows. Among those buried in the pretty churchyard are Alexander Hamilton and Robert Fulton. ⏱ *25 min. 79 Broadway (at Wall St.). www.trinity wallstreet.org. ☎ 212/602-0800. Mon–Fri 7am–6pm, Sat 8am–4pm, Sun 7am–4pm. Subway: 4/5 to Wall St.*

❹ ★ **Eataly.** The hugely popular all-Italian food hall opened a downtown branch in late 2016. Grab a quick but expertly crafted panini or have a full sit-down meal. *101 Liberty St., 3rd floor (just off Broadway). www. eataly.com. ☎ 212/897-2895. $–$$.*

❺ ★★ **St. Paul's Chapel.** Manhattan's only surviving pre-Revolutionary church was built in 1766 to resemble London's St. Martin-in-the-Fields. George Washington

Trinity Church's cemetery, where founding father Alexander Hamilton is buried.

came here to pray right after his inauguration as the first president of the United States. With a light, elegant Georgian interior, the chapel was a refuge for rescue workers after September 11; you'll see exhibits and artifacts from that dark period. ⏲ *25 min. 209 Broadway (at Fulton St.). www.trinitywallstreet.org.* ☎ *212/233-4164. Mon–Fri 10am–6pm, Sat 10am–4pm, Sun 7am–3pm. Subway: 2/3 to Park Place; 1/9/4/5/A to Fulton St./Broadway/Nassau.*

⑥ ★★★ 9/11 Memorial and Museum. The Twin Towers dominated the Manhattan skyline after their construction in 1973, and visitors from around the world have made pilgrimages to this site since their destruction during the September 11, 2001, terrorist attacks. A permanent memorial, *Reflecting Absence*, converts the footprints of the Twin Towers into large reflective pools, incorporating the largest man-made waterfalls in North America. On the same plaza is the 9/11 Museum, a powerful and emotional retelling of the attacks on the towers, the Pentagon, and United Airlines Flight 93 in Pennsylvania. The museum uses artifacts, video and audio recordings, photography, interactive panels and more, to create a sophisticated, multidimensional history lesson, one that may be too intense for children under 12. *Tip:* Guided tours of the museum are available for an additional cost, but we think most visitors will prefer the self-guided tour. ⏲ *2 hr. Entrances at intersections of Liberty and Greenwich sts., Liberty and West sts, or West and Fulton sts. www.911memorial.org.* ☎ *212/266-5211. Museum admission $24; $18 seniors, U.S. veterans, and students; $15 children 7–17; free on Tuesdays 5–8pm. Memorial park open daily*

One World Trade Center.

7:30am–9pm; museum open Sun–Thurs 9am–8pm and Fri–Sat 9am–9pm. Subway: A/C/J/Z, 2/3, or 4/5 to Fulton St., 2/3 to Park Place, A/C/E to World Trade Center, R to Rector St., N/R to Cortland St.

⑦ ★ One World Observatory. Architect Daniel Libeskind's 1,776-foot-tall (533m) **One World Trade Center** is the tallest building in North America, and near its apex is, you guessed it, the tallest observatory on this side of the planet. You can see for miles through its floor-to-ceiling windows, but because you're kept inside, and because the building is on the tip of Manhattan, rather than in its heart, we don't think it has the visceral thrill of the Empire State Building. Still, if you missed going up that, this is a worthy second choice. *1 World Trade (entrance on Vesey St. at West St.). http://one worldobservatory.com.* ☎ *844/696-1776. Basic admission $32 adults; $30 seniors, $26 children. Early May to early Sept daily 9am–10pm,*

9am–8pm rest of year. Subway: A, C, J, Z, 2, 3, 4, or 5 to Fulton St., 2, 3 to Park Place, E to World Trade Center, R to Rector St., Subway: A/C to World Trade Center, N/R to Cortland St.

❽ ★ World Trade Center Transportation Hub.

The only subway stop in the city that's now an attraction in its own right, this winglike steel and glass canopy, designed by Catalan architect Santiago Calatrava, is an extraordinary work of architecture. *Tip:* If you stand on Broadway, you can get a photo of One World Trade Center rising up between its arms. *At the intersection of Fulton and Church St.*

❾ City Hall Park.

City Hall has been the seat of NYC government since 1812. Individual tours of the inside are available Thursdays at 10am, but if that's not an option, you can appreciate the handsome park, highlighted by flickering gaslight lamps, and the 1811 building's French Renaissance exterior. Abraham Lincoln was laid in state in the soaring rotunda. Equally grand is the colossal **Municipal Building** (1 Centre St. at Chambers St.), built on the other side of Centre Street in 1915 by McKim, Mead & White; it was the celebrated firm's first "skyscraper." Across Broadway at no. 233 is that temple of commerce known as the ★★ **Woolworth Building.** Built from the proceeds of a nickel-and-dime empire in 1913, this gargoyle-laden masterpiece is the work of Cass Gilbert. Near-daily tours of the lobby are now offered, thanks to the efforts of Gilbert's great-granddaughter. *City Hall Park (btw. Broadway and Park Row). Woolworth building $20–$30 tours, depending on length. www.woolworthtours.com.*

❿ ★ Foley Square.

It's hard to believe that this dignified urban landscape was once a fetid swamp and, in the 19th century, one of the city's most notorious slums, Five Points. Today, with its ring of colonnaded courthouse buildings, Foley Square bustles with judiciary industry. It's also one of the most filmed places in the five boroughs. The exterior of the 1913 **NY State Supreme Court Building** (60 Centre St.) is where Kris Kringle goes on trial in *Miracle on 34th Street* (the original) and also looks very familiar if you are a *Law & Order* fan. The imposing 1932 **Thurgood Marshall U.S. Courthouse** (40 Centre St.) was designed by Cass Gilbert. *Bounded by Centre, Worth and Lafayette sts. Subway: 4/5/6 to Brooklyn Bridge/City Hall.*

⓫ ★ The Dead Rabbit Grocery and Grog.

Grab a punch, a flip, a nog or some other historically accurate 19th century cocktail at this charmingly old-timey bar, which was named best bar in the world in 2016, by the mixologists who put together the influential "50 Best Bars" list. A light (but tasty) supper is served. *30 Water St. (near Broad St.). www.deadrabbitnyc.com.* ☎ 212/897-2895. $–$$. ●

2 The Best Special-Interest Tours

Romantic New York

1 Neue Gallery
2 The Lake
3 Picnic in the Sheep Meadow
4 The Plaza
5 Tiffany & Co
6 Summer on the Lincoln Center Plaza
7 Winter on the Rink in Rockefeller Center
8 The Whispering Gallery
9 The Museum of Sex
10 Mimi
11 One if By Land, Two if By Sea
12 Harbor Cruise
13 The River Café

Previous page: Walk across the Brooklyn Bridge for panoramic skyline views.

New York is known for its wolves of Wall Street and other all-business movers-and-shakers. But to me, the city harbors a romantic streak as wide as the Hudson River. Here are some places best discovered as a twosome. START: **Subway 4, 5, or 6 to 86th Street.**

Minne sculptures and a Klimt painting in the Neue Galerie.

❶ ★★ Neue Galerie New York.

If you don't think museums can be sexy, you haven't visited the Neue, which does not allow anyone younger than 13 to see its sometimes risqué collection of Austrian and German art from 1890 to 1940. Not only does the Galerie house some of Gustave Klimt's most sensual works (including the famed "Woman in Gold"), it's set in an opulent 1912 mansion, designed by the team of Carrere & Hastings, and has a soigné, wood-paneled, Viennese-style cafe perfect for canoodling. The cafe becomes a cabaret on Thursday evenings, attracting some of the top performers in the biz. *1048 Fifth Ave. (at 86th St.). www.neuegalerie.org.* ☎ *212/628-6200. Admission $20 adults, $15 seniors, $10 students. Thurs–Mon 11am–6pm.*

❷ ★★ The Lake.

When you see the shimmering waters edged by weeping willows and Japanese cherry trees, you'll understand why it inspired songwriters Rodgers and

Rowing on Central Park Lake.

Hart ("I love the rowing on Central Park Lake" in "The Lady Is a Tramp"). The green banks along the man-made lake slope gently toward the water and make for an ideal picnic spot. You can rent a rowboat for two at the neo-Victorian Loeb Boathouse at the east end of the lake. The boathouse also has a restaurant and a seasonal outside bar with seating overlooking the lake. It's a thoroughly pleasant place to enjoy a cool summer cocktail. *Midpark from 71st to 78th sts.*

❸ **Sheep Meadow.** Skip the horse-drawn carriage rides, which are pretty pricey (roughly $50 for 20 min.). Head to the Sheep Meadow instead, a large green swath in lower Central Park that, yes, was once a grazing ground. It's got stupendous views of the Central Park South skyline pillowed in trees, perfect for a picnic. *Midpark btw. 66th and 69th sts.*

❹ ★★ **The Plaza.** This historic confection of a hotel has fueled countless romances. Newlyweds Scott and Zelda Fitzgerald famously frolicked in the fountain out front. And who can forget the poignant final scene in *The Way We Were*, when Barbra Streisand and Robert Redford say good-bye in front of the Plaza? The scene was lovingly re-created on TV's *Sex and the City*. Toast to bittersweet romance in the swank Champagne Bar. *768 Fifth Ave. (at 59th St.). www. theplazany.com.* ☎ *212/759-3000. Subway: N/R/W to Fifth Ave. and 59th St.*

❺ ★★ **Tiffany & Co.** Grab a croissant and a coffee and make like Audrey Hepburn in *Breakfast at Tiffany's*. Or just wander through, admiring all the sparkly stuff at this classic jewelry shop. You don't need to buy to enjoy Tiffany's. *727 Fifth Ave. (btw. 56th and 57th sts.).*

☎ *212/755-8000. Subway: E/M to Fifth Ave./53rd St.*

❻ **Lincoln Center Plaza.** On a warm summer night, grab your partner and dance with abandon during "Midsummer Night Swing," the sexy dance party on Josie Robertson Plaza. Every night is a different dance theme, from salsa to swing to ballroom. The fountains and floodlights of the plaza are particularly seductive at dusk. *Columbus Ave. at 64th St. www. lincolncenter.org. See p 145.*

❼ ★★ **The Rink in Rockefeller Center.** A romantic winter rendezvous on the ice-skating rink in the center's Lower Plaza is clichéd, but just try to resist a swirl around the ice during the holidays, with the spectacular Rock Center Christmas tree glittering from above. Avoid crowds by going early or late. Don't skate? Have a drink in the Sea Grill—which directly faces the rink—and watch the action. *Lower Plaza, Rockefeller Center (btw. 49th and 50th sts.).* ☎ *212/332-7654. Admission $25 adults, $15 seniors and children 11 and under; skate rental $12. Mid-Oct to mid-Apr; daily 8:30am–midnight. See p 8.*

❽ **The Whispering Gallery.** Not only is the tiled Gustavino ceiling outside the Grand Central Oyster Bar a beauty, but it creates an acoustical phenomenon. Stand facing one of the pillars with your loved one facing the one directly opposite and whisper sweet nothings. You'll be able to hear one another—and no one else can listen in. *Grand Central Station, 42nd St. and Park Ave. www.grandcentral terminal.com.* ☎ *212/340-2210. Subway: 4/5/6 to 42nd St./Grand Central.*

❾ ★ **Museum of Sex.** OK, so we're stretching the definition of

Skaters on the Rockefeller Center skating rink.

romance with this one. But heck, a visit to this repository of early sex films, S&M displays, painted nudes, blow-up dolls, and other paraphernalia could make your time back at the hotel a bit more interesting. ⏱ *1 hr. 233 Fifth Ave. (at 27th St.). www.museumofsex.com.* ☎ *212/ 689-6337. Admission $18 adults, $15 students and seniors. No one under 18 admitted. Sun–Thurs 10am–8pm, Fri–Sat 10am–9pm. Subway: N/R to 28th St.*

⑩ ★★★ Mimi. Dining at this tiny Greenwich Village bistro, with its dappled marble wall and sleek Art Deco styling, would be an aphrodisiac even if the food weren't spectacular. But it is, a daringly original take on classic French cuisine by 26-year-old rising star chef Liz Johnson. *185 Sullivan St. (near Houston). www.miminyc.com.* ☎ *212/418-01260. $$$$.*

⑪ ★ One If By Land, Two If By Sea. The former carriage house of Vice President Aaron Burr (Alexander Hamilton's killer) makes the perfect setting for popping the question. Lit by crystal chandeliers and suffused with historic charm, it has a menu as classy as the setting. *17 Barrow St. (btw. Seventh Ave. and West 4th St.) www.oneifbyland.com. $$$$.*

⑫ ★★ Harbor Cruise. Whether you're on a simple spin around the island or an elegant dinner cruise, seeing Manhattan from the water is a thrill. That old reliable, **Circle Line** (www.circleline42.com), has the most options, from 2-hour harbor cruises to sunset harbor lights cruises, from $38 to $42. Circle Line leaves from Pier 83 (W. 42nd St.). **Bateaux New York** (www.bateaux newyork.com) runs dinner cruises in sleek glass boats to the accompaniment of live jazz, from $98 to $140. It leaves from Pier 61 at Chelsea Piers (W. 23rd St.).

⑬ ★ The River Café. The River Café sits on the Brooklyn waterfront practically underneath the Brooklyn Bridge, with magnificent views of downtown Manhattan. Even if you don't come for dinner, you can sit on the terrace, sip a cocktail, and drink in the views. *1 Water St., Brooklyn. www.rivercafe.com.* ☎ *718/522-5200. $$$–$$$$.*

New York with Kids

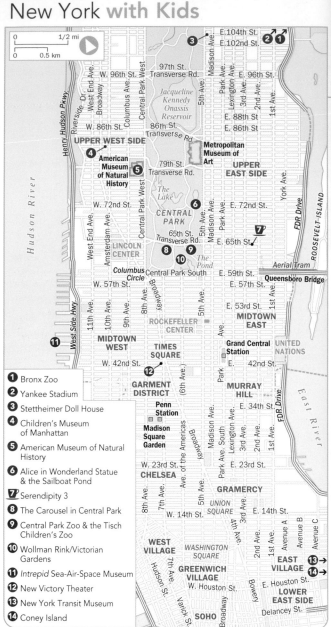

1. Bronx Zoo
2. Yankee Stadium
3. Stettheimer Doll House
4. Children's Museum of Manhattan
5. American Museum of Natural History
6. Alice in Wonderland Statue & the Sailboat Pond
7. Serendipity 3
8. The Carousel in Central Park
9. Central Park Zoo & the Tisch Children's Zoo
10. Wollman Rink/Victorian Gardens
11. Intrepid Sea-Air-Space Museum
12. New Victory Theater
13. New York Transit Museum
14. Coney Island

Beneath its noise, grit, and air of jaded cynicism, New York City is extremely kid-friendly. It opens its arms to kids of all ages, with some of the top children's attractions in the country, magical kid-centric holidays, and a world of treats for the eyes, ears, and tummy. What kid can resist? Just be sure to budget 3 to 4 days if you want to fit in everything on this tour. START: **Subway 2 or 5 to East Tremont Avenue/West Farms Square.**

❶ ★★★ 🄺🄸🄳🅂 **Bronx Zoo.** The largest urban wildlife conservation facility in America, the Bronx Zoo has some 4,000 animals roaming 265 acres (106 hectares). It's hard to believe that you're actually in the Bronx as you watch lions, zebras, and gazelles roam the African Plains, a re-created savanna. Other highlights: Tiger Mountain (Siberian tigers), and the Congo Gorilla Forest, where 23 lowland gorillas, assorted monkeys, and other species live in a 6½-acre (2.6-hectare) African rainforest environment. ⏲ 1–5 hr. *Fordham Rd. and Bronx River Pkwy. www.bronxzoo.com.* ☎ *718/652-8400. Mon–Fri 10am–4:30pm, Sat–Sun 10am–5:30pm (extended summer and holiday hours). Admission $34 adults, $29 seniors, $24 children 3–12, free for kids 2 and under. Subway: 2/5 to E. Tremont Ave./W. Farms Sq.*

❷ ★★ 🄺🄸🄳🅂 **Yankee Stadium.** Is there a better way to spend a sun-dappled afternoon or warm summer evening than at a baseball game at Yankee Stadium? And the quickest and most convenient way to get to the stadium is the subway. ⏲ 4 hr. *1 E. 161st St. (Jerome Ave.), the Bronx. www.yankees.com.* ☎ *718/293-6000. Tickets $15–$65. Subway: B/D/4 to 161st St.*

❸ ★ 🄺🄸🄳🅂 **Stettheimer Doll House.** This remarkable dollhouse in the **Museum of the City of New York** was the creation of Carrie Walter Stettheimer, a theater set designer who, with her two equally talented sisters, entertained the

city's avant-garde artist community in the 1920s. Among the exquisite furnishings are period wallpaper, paper lampshades, and an art gallery featuring miniatures of such famous works as Marcel Duchamp's *Nude Descending a Staircase.* The museum has more vintage dollhouses and timeless toys on display. ⏲ 1½ hr. *Museum of the City of New York, 1220 Fifth Ave. (103rd St.). www.mcny.org.* ☎ *212/534-1672. Tues–Sun 10am–5pm. Admission $14 adults, $10 seniors, free for children 19 and under. Subway: 6 to 103rd St.*

❹ ★★ 🄺🄸🄳🅂 **Children's Museum of Manhattan.** A rambling, indoor/outdoor fun house (shhh . . . it's also educational), CMOM entertains everyone from toddlers to ten-year-olds with interactive science experiments, daily shows, water features, playrooms, and changing exhibits on

Sea lions at the Bronx Zoo.

everything from ancient Greece to the art of Andy Warhol. ⏱ *2 hr. Children's Museum of Manhattan, 212 W. 83rd St. (btw Broadway and Amsterdam.). www.cmom.org.* ☎ *212/721-1223. Sun–Fri 10am–5pm, Sat 10am–7pm. Admission $12 adults and children, $8 seniors. Subway: 1 to 86th St.*

❺ ★★★ kids American Museum of Natural History.

One word: ★ **dinosaurs,** which devour the entrance hall and take up the entire fourth floor. Not to mention diamonds as big as the Ritz, and much more. *See p 50.*

❻ ★★ kids Central Park's Alice in Wonderland Statue & Sailboat Pond.

The 1959 bronze statue of Alice sitting on a giant mushroom becomes one big jungle gym in warm weather. Next to it is Conservatory Water, an ornamental pond where kids sail miniature boats (rented on site). *Central Park, east side from 72nd to 75th sts.*

7 kids Serendipity 3.

The Frr-rozen Hot Chocolate is legendary at this whimsical Upper East Side dessert parlor, which also serves kid-friendly burgers, pastas, and chicken potpie. *225 E. 60th St. (btw. Second and Third aves.). www.serendipity3.com.* ☎ *212/838-3531. $$.*

❽ ★★ kids The Carousel in Central Park.

A quarter of a million children ride these vintage hand-carved horses every year. *See p 103.*

❾ ★★ kids Central Park Zoo.

Built in 1988 to replace a 1934 WPA-built structure, the zoo's 5½ acres (2.2 hectare) house more than 400 animals, among them sea lions, polar bears, and penguins. In the small **Tisch Children's Zoo,** kids can feed and pet tame farm animals. Check out the **Delacorte**

Clock, with six dancing animals designed by the Italian sculptor Andrea Spadini. *See p 103.*

❿ ★★ kids Wollman Rink/ Victorian Gardens.

Central Park's spacious rink is built for stretching out and perfecting your moves. Plus, it has views of skyscrapers along Central Park South. In summer, it's transformed into the **Victorian Gardens Amusement Park,** which has old-fashioned carnival rides. *See p 103.*

⓫ ★★★ kids Intrepid Sea, Air & Space.

The aircraft carrier known as the "Fighting I" served the U.S. Navy for 31 years, suffering bomb attacks, kamikaze strikes, and a torpedo shot. It's now a very cool sea, air, and space museum on the waterfront. You can crawl inside a wooden sub from the American Revolution, inspect a missile submarine, manipulate the controls in the cockpit of an A-6 Intruder and view an actual space shuttle. ⏱ *1½ hr. Pier 86, 12th Ave. and 46th St. http://intrepidmuseum.org.* ☎ *212/245-0072. Admission $24 adults, $20 students and seniors, $19 children 3–17, free for children 2 and under. Apr–Sept Mon–Fri 10am–5pm, Sat–Sun 10am–6pm; Oct–Mar Tues–Sun 10am–5pm. Bus: M42 to 12th St. and Hudson Ave. Subway: 1/2/3/7/9/A/C/E/S to 42nd St./ Times Sq.*

⓬ ★★ New Victory Theater.

Imaginative, kid-appropriate shows from around the globe play here—musicals, circuses, puppet shows, dance, you name it. Many of its offerings over the years have been wondrous. ⏱ *2 hr. 209 W. 42nd St. (off Broadway).* ☎ *646-223-3010. Tickets start at $16. Subway: 1/2/3/7/9/ A/C/E/S to 42nd St./Times Sq*

⓭ ★ kids New York Transit Museum.

Cool vintage turnstiles and subway trains that the little

The New Victory Theater presents kid-friendly shows like Mother Africa; My Home.

ones can scramble all over are the centerpiece of this underground museum, set in an abandoned station. *Boerum Place and Schermerhorn St., Brooklyn www.nytransitmuseum.org.* ☎ *718/694-1600. Admission $7 adults, $5 seniors and children 2–17. Tues–Fri 10am–4pm; Sat–Sun 11am–5pm. Subway: A, C to Hoyt St.; F to Jay St.; M, R to Court St.; 2, 3, 4, 5 to Borough Hall.*

⓮ ★ kids **Coney Island.** This classic summer playground has carny rides, wooden boardwalks, and breezy salt air. It's a long subway ride out, but once you're here you can ride the 1927 **Cyclone** roller coaster or the 1920 **Wonder Wheel;** play at **Luna Park,** the first new amusement park built on Coney Island in 40 years; or splash in the sea. *1208 Surf Ave., Brooklyn. www.coneyisland.com; www.lunaparknyc.com.* ☎ *718/372-5159. Ride prices vary. Memorial Day to Labor Day daily noon to late evening; Easter to Memorial Day and Labor Day to end of Oct weekends noon to late evening. Subway: D/N to Coney Island/Stillwell Ave.; F/Q to W. 8th St.*

Holiday Magic

New York celebrates the holidays with glitter and gusto. On Thanksgiving, the **Macy's Day Parade** rolls through town; wake up early to find yourself a perch along the parade route. Join the locals the night before for a street party around the Museum of Natural History to watch the giant parade balloons being inflated. From November through early January, the ever-popular **Christmas Spectacular** (www.radiocity.com; ☎ 212/307-1000; tickets $49–$250) plays at Radio City Music Hall, while in the Bronx, the New York Botanical Gardens mounts the wonderful **Holiday Train Show,** where vintage model trains zip around miniature reproductions of New York landmarks—all made *entirely out of plant materials* (www.nybg.org; ☎ 718/817-8700; $20 adults, $18 seniors and students, $8 children 2–12; take Metro-North Railroad from Grand Central to the Botanical Gardens stop).

Literary Gotham

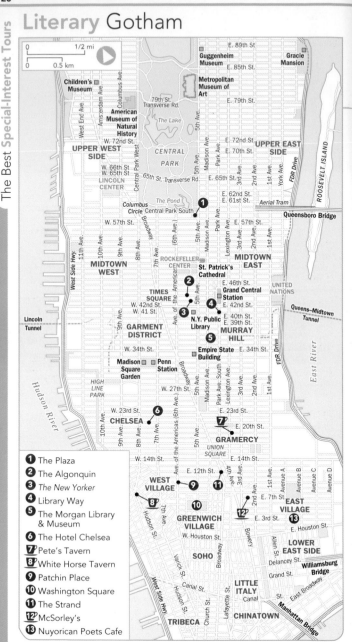

0 | 1/2 mi
0 | 0.5 km

Children's Museum

Guggenheim Museum

Gracie Mansion

E. 89th St.

E. 85th St.

Metropolitan Museum of Art

E. 79th St.

79th St. Transverse Rd.

American Museum of Natural History

W. 72nd St.

The Lake

E. 72nd St.

UPPER EAST SIDE

E. 70th St.

UPPER WEST SIDE

W. 66th St
W. 65th St

CENTRAL PARK

E. 65th St.

LINCOLN CENTER

65th St. Transverse Rd.

ROOSEVELT ISLAND

FDR Drive

Columbus Circle

The Pond

Central Park South

E. 62nd St.
E. 61st St.

Aerial Tram

❶

W. 57th St.

E. 57th St.

Queensboro Bridge

ROCKEFELLER CENTER

MIDTOWN WEST

MIDTOWN EAST

St. Patrick's Cathedral

E. 46th St.

Grand Central Station

❷

TIMES SQUARE

W. 42nd St.
W. 41 St.

E. 42nd St.

❸ **❹**

E. 40th St.
E. 39th St.

N.Y. Public Library

❺

UNITED NATIONS

Queens–Midtown Tunnel

Lincoln Tunnel

GARMENT DISTRICT

MURRAY HILL

W. 34th St.

Empire State Building

E. 34th St.

Madison Square Garden

Penn Station

FDR Drive

HIGH LINE PARK

W. 27th St.

East River

W. 23rd St.

❻

E. 23rd St.

CHELSEA

❼

E. 20th St.

GRAMERCY

UNION SQUARE

W. 14th St.

E. 14th St.

❾ **⓫**

W. 12th St.

E. 12th St.

WEST VILLAGE

EAST VILLAGE

❽

❿

E. 7th St.

⓬

GREENWICH VILLAGE

E. 3rd St.

E. Houston St.

W. Houston St.

SOHO

LOWER EAST SIDE

Delancey St.

Williamsburg Bridge

Grand St.

LITTLE ITALY

Canal St.

East Broadway

TRIBECA

CHINATOWN

Manhattan Bridge

Hudson River

West Side Hwy.

Legend

❶ The Plaza
❷ The Algonquin
❸ *The New Yorker*
❹ Library Way
❺ The Morgan Library & Museum
❻ The Hotel Chelsea
❼ Pete's Tavern
❽ White Horse Tavern
❾ Patchin Place
❿ Washington Square
⓫ The Strand
⓬ McSorley's
⓭ Nuyorican Poets Cafe

There is something about New York life that has long inspired writers. The home of the publishing industry, New York is a town that embraces the written word. Readings by big-name as well as undiscovered authors are a daily occurrence at venues throughout the city. What follows is a tour of some of the city's past and present literary landmarks (we have more in our tour of Greenwich Village, p 68). **START: N, R, or W to Fifth Avenue and 59th Street.**

❶ ★★ The Plaza. Eloise lived here, of course; the celebrated children's book heroine won the hotel "Literary Landmark" status in 1998. *Eloise* was written in 1955 by performer Kay Thompson during her stay at the Plaza, and the famous portrait of the mischievous little girl is still displayed in the renovated lobby. *See p 9.*

❷ ★ The Algonquin. In the 1920s, this hotel was where such notable literati as James Thurber and the acid-tongued Dorothy Parker met to drink and trade bons mots at the so-called Round Table (the hotel's restaurant now takes that name). Alas, both the restaurant and lobby have been stripped of their original décor/ambiance. *59 W. 44th St. (btw. Fifth and Sixth aves.). www. algonquinhotel.com.* ☎ *212/840-6800. Subway: B/D/F/M to 42nd St.*

❸ The former *New Yorker* offices. America's most celebrated literary magazine came into being at the Algonquin Round Table, just a block away from its former office space here. Over the decades, it has featured such writers as E. B. White, John Cheever, John Updike, and Calvin Trillin, and you'll find their names and others on a plaque. *25 W. 43rd St. (btw. Fifth and Sixth aves.). Subway: B/D/ F/M to 42nd St.*

❹ ★ Library Way. Along 41st Street between Park and Fifth, 96 bronze plaques embedded in the sidewalk all feature quotations from literature or poetry. Walking west along this street leads you to the legendary New York Public Library (p 8). *41st St. (btw. Park and Fifth aves.). Subway: B/D/F/M to 42nd St.*

❺ ★★ The Morgan Library & Museum. The former private library of financier John Pierpont Morgan contains one of the world's

East Room of the Morgan Library and Museum.

most important collections of rare books and manuscripts. It was not Morgan himself who bartered with booksellers but his personal librarian, Belle da Costa Greene, a light-skinned African American who passed herself off as white to gain entree into Morgan's world. For more than 40 years, Morgan gave her carte blanche (money was no object) to build the collection. In addition to displaying these treasures (usually a Gutenberg bible is on view), the museum creates special exhibitions on such topics as Emily Dickinson's works or the writings and images of Martin Luther. ⓧ *2 hr. 29 E. 36th St. (btw. Park and Madison aves.). www.themorgan.org.* ☎ *212/685-0610. Admission $20 adults, $13 seniors, students and children 13–15, free children for 12 and under. Tues–Thurs 10:30am–5pm, Fri 10:30am–9pm, Sat 10am–6pm, Sun 11am–6pm. Subway: B/D/F/N/Q/R/M to 34th St.*

❻ The Hotel Chelsea. Built in 1884, the Chelsea became a hotel in 1905 where artists and writers were encouraged to stay indefinitely. Among the writers who did: Mark Twain, Thomas Wolfe, Dylan Thomas, O. Henry, Arthur Miller, and Sam Shepard (with his then-lover Patti Smith). The hotel is closed, used primarily now for film and television production, but you can still admire its grandeur from outside. *222 W. 23rd St. (btw. Seventh and Eighth aves.). www. hotelchelsea.com.* ☎ *212/243-3700. Subway: 1/9/A/C to 23rd St.*

❼ Pete's Tavern. Literary ghosts abound at ancient Pete's Tavern, a New York City landmark that claims to be the oldest continuing dining establishment in New York (1864). In the second booth from the front writer O. Henry is said to have penned his Christmas fable Gift of the Magi in 1906. In 1939, writer Ludwig Bemelmans used Pete's Tavern as his office to write the first in his Madeline children's book series. These days, instead of thirsty cash-strapped writers, you are more likely to see film crews in and around Pete's trying to re-create that old literary New York look. *129 E. 18th Street (at Irving Plaza). www.petes tavern.com.* ☎ *212/473-7676. $$.*

❽ White Horse Tavern. This 1880 wood-frame bar was where such writers as Jack Kerouac, James Baldwin, Norman Mailer, and the Welsh poet Dylan Thomas threw down a few. Thomas, in fact, more or less drank himself to death here in November 1953 at the tender age of 39. Order a newfangled burger, wash it down with an icy ale, and toast the celebrated ghosts around you. Cash only. *567 Hudson St. (at 11th St.).* ☎ *212/243-9260. $–$$.*

❾ Patchin Place. This sweet little cobblestone mews tucked off Sixth Avenue was at one time a serious literary enclave: The poet e e cummings lived at no. 4 from 1923 to 1962, the reclusive writer Djuna Barnes lived at no. 5 for 40 years, and journalist John Reed and his paramour Louise Bryant lived here while he wrote *Ten Days That Shook the World.* (The lefty magazine he wrote for, *The Masses,* had its office a couple of blocks away at 91 Greenwich Ave.) *Patchin Place (off 10th St. and Sixth Ave.). Subway: A/B/C/D/E/F/M to W. 4th St.*

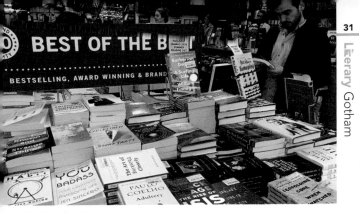

The Strand Bookstore.

⓾ Washington Square. The literary history of New York is filled with references to this fabled downtown neighborhood—and why not? It's where many great writers grew up or chose to live. Novelist Henry James was born at 21 Washington Place in 1843 and later described the neighborhood in his memorable 1880 book *Washington Square* (later made into the heralded play and movie *The Heiress*). Edith Wharton, whose novels evoked the genteel days when the aristocracy ruled New York society from Washington Square, stayed briefly with her mother at 7 Washington Sq. N.

McSorley's Old Ale House.

Willa Cather lived at both 60 Washington Sq. S. and 82 Washington Place. *See p 69.*

⓫ ★ The Strand. You can spend hours browsing the "18 miles" of new and used books crammed into the high, narrow shelves of this 1927 institution/bookstore. *See p 91.*

⓬ McSorley's. This working 1854 saloon was immortalized by New Yorker writer Joseph Mitchell in "McSorley's Wonderful Saloon," found in his classic collection of true New York tales, Up in the Old Hotel and Other Stories. *15 E. 7th St. (btw. Second and Third aves.). www.mcsorleysnewyork.com.* ☎ *212/474-9148. $.*

⓭ Nuyorican Poets Cafe. What started out more than 30 years ago as the "living room salon" of East Village writer and poet Miguel Algarín has become a celebrated arts enterprise and a forum for up and-coming poets, writers, playwrights, musicians, and comedians. Weekly poetry slams are held Friday nights. *236 E. 3rd St. (btw. aves. B and C). www.nuyorican.org.* ☎ *212/505-8183. Subway: A/B/C/D/ E/F/M to W. 4th St.*

New York's Unforgettable Architecture

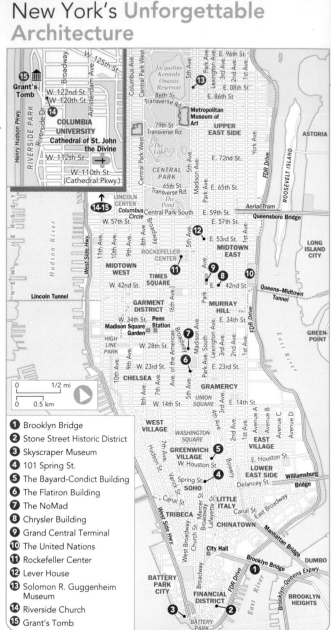

1. Brooklyn Bridge
2. Stone Street Historic District
3. Skyscraper Museum
4. 101 Spring St.
5. The Bayard-Condict Building
6. The Flatiron Building
7. The NoMad
8. Chrysler Building
9. Grand Central Terminal
10. The United Nations
11. Rockefeller Center
12. Lever House
13. Solomon R. Guggenheim Museum
14. Riverside Church
15. Grant's Tomb

M anhattan's muscular skyline is many things: an eclectic architectural landscape; a visual metaphor for the dynamism of America's largest city, perpetually in flux; and a stunning, three-dimensional historical record of how the Big Apple has grown—and grown up—over the years. This tour takes in a bit of all that, in 2 days. START: Subway 4, 5, or 6 to Brooklyn Bridge/City Hall.

❶ ★★★ Brooklyn Bridge. It took 16 very difficult years to build, but in 1883 this architectural and engineering marvel was finally finished. The 20- to 40-minute stroll on the bridge's wood-planked walkway is one of New York's must-do activities. Not only is the bridge a wonder to behold, but the views of Manhattan from it are equally stunning. *Subway: 4/5/6 to Brooklyn Bridge–City Hall.*

❷ ★ Stone Street Historic District. This narrow cobblestone street was staked out by the Dutch West India Company in the 1640s. The 15 brick structures that line it were all built in the year after the Great Fire of 1835 leveled the heavily commercial neighborhood, making this one of the most historically cohesive streets in the city. The street is closed to vehicular traffic and filled with the outdoor tables

Historic Stone Street.

of the taverns and cafes that now inhabit these former warehouses (it's a real party scene in the warmer weather months). *Bounded by Pearl St., Hanover Sq., S. William St. and Coenties Alley. Subway: 2/3 to Wall St.*

❸ ★ Skyscraper Museum. Wowed by New York's sheer verticality? Learn more about the technology, culture, and muscle behind it all at this tiny museum. It contains two galleries: one dedicated to the evolution of Manhattan's skyline, and the other to changing shows. ⏱ *1 hr. 2 West St. (museum entrance faces Battery Place). www.skyscraper.org. ☎ 212/968-1961. Admission $5 adults, $2.50 seniors and students, free for children 11 and under. Wed–Sun noon–6pm. Subway: 1 to Rector St; 4/5 to Bowling Green.*

❹ ★ 101 Spring Street. This five-story cast-iron building, built by architect Nicholas Whyte in 1870, remains the only intact single-use cast-iron building in SoHo. In 1968, minimalist Donald Judd (1928–1994) bought the former bowling factory and transformed it into a home and studio, now open to the public; the works on view in the building were set in place by the artist himself. Guided visits are $25 and offered Thurs–Sat and Tuesdays. Check www.juddfoundation.org for times and reservations. *101 Spring St. (btw. Prince and Mercer sts.). Subway: N/R to Prince St.*

❺ ★ The Bayard-Condict Building. Renowned Chicago architect Louis Sullivan was Frank Lloyd Wright's boss and, some say, his mentor. The only building Sullivan designed in New York is hidden down a nondescript NoHo street. It's a beaut, nonetheless: Constructed in 1899, the 13-story building is a creamy confection, with fanciful terra-cotta decoration and ornamental friezes. *65 Bleecker St. (btw. Broadway and Lafayette St.). Subway: 6 to Bleecker St.*

❻ ★★★ The Flatiron Building. This triangular masterpiece is one of the city's most distinctive silhouettes. Its pie-slice form was the solution to a problem—filling the wedge of land created by the intersection of Fifth Avenue and Broadway. Built in 1902, the Flatiron measures only 6 feet (1.8m) across at its narrow end. So called for its resemblance to the laundry appliance, it was originally named the Fuller Building, then later "Burnham's Folly" because people were certain that architect Daniel Burnham's 21-story structure would fall down. The building mainly houses publishing offices, but it has a few shops on the ground floor. The surrounding neighborhood has taken its name—the Flatiron District, home to smart restaurants and shops. *175 Fifth Ave. (at 23rd St.). Subway: R to 23rd St.*

❼ The Nomad. Architectural Digest named this one of the most "beautifully designed" restaurants in the world, and you'll understand why once you're seated under its pyramidal glass-roofed atrium or next to the ornate and massive fireplace (imported from a French chateau). The gourmet American fare is as sumptuous as the decor. 1170 Broadway (at 28th St.). *www.the nomadhotel.com/dining.* ☎ 212/ 796-1500. $$$$.

The Flatiron Building.

❽ ★★★ Chrysler Building. This 1930 Art Deco masterpiece was designed to be the world's tallest building—and it was, if only for a year. In the race against other New York architects to build the tallest skyscraper of the era, William Van Alen secretly added a stainless-steel spire inside the fire shaft, hoisting it into place only after his competitors thought his building was completed. *405 Lexington Ave. (at 42nd St.). Subway: 4/5/6 to Grand Central.*

❾ ★★★ Grand Central Terminal. This magnificent public space is also an engineering wonder. The "elevated circumferential plaza," as it was called in 1913, splits Park Avenue, which is diverted around the building. The network of trains—subway and commuter—that pass through here is vast, but even more impressive is the "bridge" over the tracks, designed to support a cluster of skyscrapers. The main concourse was restored to its original glory in 1998; the *Sky*

Grand Central Terminal's soaring main concourse.

Ceiling inside depicts the constellations of the winter sky above New York. They're lit with 59 stars surrounded by dazzling 24-karat gold.

The United Nations headquarters.

Emitting light fed through fiber-optic cables, the stars in their intensities roughly replicate the magnitude of the actual stars as seen from Earth. Look carefully and you'll see a patch near one corner left unrestored—a reminder of the neglect this splendid masterpiece once endured. *42nd St. and Park Ave. www.grandcentralterminal.com. ☎ 212/340-2210. Subway: 4/5/6/7/S to 42nd St.*

🔟 ★★ **The United Nations.** In keeping with the mission of this body, the United Nations complex was designed by an international team, spearheaded by Le Corbusier of France and Oscar Niermeyer of Brazil. Ironically, the institution created to advance the cause of world peace was built upon the grounds of slaughterhouses (the area was known as "Blood Alley"). All of the buildings (erected between 1948 and 1952) were done in the sleek "International" style, appropriately enough. Fascinating tours lead

Rockefeller Center

S, 4, 5, 6, 7 to 42nd St./Grand Central.

⓫ ★★★ Rockefeller Center. Rock Center was erected at the height of the Great Depression and, by many estimates, kept the city afloat—the nine-year construction employed 75,000 New Yorkers. The focal point is the soaring 70-story **GE Building** at 30 Rockefeller Plaza, which John D. Rockefeller said represented humanity's ability to break new frontiers. Its entrance sculpture, *Wisdom*, by Lee Lawrie, is an Art Deco masterpiece, as is the artist's *Atlas*, at the entrance court of the International Building. The sunken plaza in front of 30 Rock is overseen by the gilded statue *Prometheus* by Paul Manship. *See p 8.*

⓬ ★ Lever House. Built in 1952, this High Modern hymn to glass has undergone a spiffy renovation to restore its original sparkle. The clean-lined, relatively small skyscraper was the first in New York to employ the "curtain wall" design philosophy, with a brilliant blue-green glass facade. *400 Park Ave. (btw. 53rd and 54th sts.). Subway: 6 to Lexington Ave.*

visitors through the lobby, the domed General Assembly chamber, and several other areas. Every member nation has donated a work of art to the complex. *Entrance First Ave. and 47th St. http://visit.un.org.* ☎ *212/963-8687. Tours $22 adults, $15 seniors and students, $13 children 5–12. Children 4 and under not permitted. Weekday tours 9am–4:30pm; weekends Visitor Center access only, 10am–4:30pm. Subway:*

Contemporary Masterpieces

If you are a fan of today's architecture, New York has more than its share. Check out Frank Gehry's curvaceous 76-story skyscraper at 1 Spruce Street in the Financial District, or his fractured white cube, the **IAC Building** at 555 W. 18th St. Just across the street from the latter is Jean Nouvelle's glass patchwork tower (at **100 Eleventh Ave.**). Look closely: every single window is a different size. There's also Calatrava's extraordinary **WTC Transportation Hub** (p 18); and in the East Village the game-changing **40 Bond Street,** which looks like a thorn forest topped by a tower.

⓭ ★★★ **Solomon R. Guggenheim Museum.** Frank Lloyd Wright's only New York edifice—built in 1959—is a brilliant feat of architecture. The Babylonian-style "inverted ziggurat" has been compared to a wedding cake or a nautilus shell, but it is full of life and movement. Just forget your fantasies about roller-skating down the ramp of the rotunda. ⏱ *1 hr. 1071 Fifth Ave. (at 89th St.). www. guggenheim.org.* ☎ *212/423-3500. Admission $22 adults, $18 seniors and students, free for children 12 and under. Sun–Wed and Fri 10am– 5:45pm, Sat 10am–7:45pm. Subway: 4/5/6 to 86th St. Bus: M1/2/3/4.*

⓮ ★ **Riverside Church.** This majestic 2-block-long Gothic church, opened in 1930, has a long history of activism and has hosted such speakers as Martin Luther King, Jr.; Nelson Mandela; and Kofi Annan. The church's soaring bell tower is the tallest in the U.S. Free tours of the church's breathtaking interiors—featuring artworks by Heinrich Hofmann—are given after Sunday services. ⏱ *1 hr. 490 Riverside Dr. (btw. 120th and 121st sts). www.theriversidechurchny.org. Subway: 1 to 116th St.*

⓯ ★ **Grant's Tomb.** This colossal mausoleum is the crown jewel of a gorgeous stretch of Riverside Park. Ulysses S. Grant, the 18th president and the commander of the Union Army, spent the last 4 years of his life in New York; he's entombed here with his wife, Julia. The deep-red twin granite sarcophagi, viewed from a circular marble mezzanine above, are a moving, almost eerie tribute to the Civil War hero. On the monument's other side is the peaceful Sakura Park, an underrated green space with a delightful Japanese feel. ⏱ *20 min. Riverside Dr. and 122nd St. www. grantstomb.org. Free admission. Summer daily 9am–5pm; spring, fall and winter Thurs–Mon 9am–5pm. Subway: 1 to 125th St.*

Frank Lloyd Wright's Guggenheim Museum.

NYC Free & Dirt-Cheap

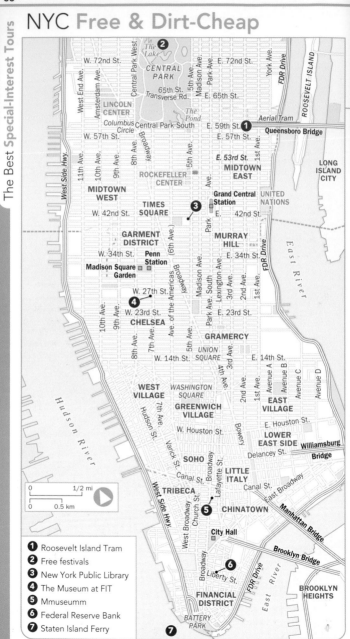

- **1** Roosevelt Island Tram
- **2** Free festivals
- **3** New York Public Library
- **4** The Museum at FIT
- **5** Mmuseumm
- **6** Federal Reserve Bank
- **7** Staten Island Ferry

Seeing the sights in New York is often just a matter of turning the corner. Brass bands wailing at Chinatown street funerals, the latest fashions parading down the catwalk that's West Bleecker Street (p 71), the animated holiday window displays at all the department stores—you won't pay a penny for any of it. Nor will you for many museums (see p 41). Here are some other free (or dirt-cheap) ways to savor the Big Apple. START: **Subway 6 to 77th or 86th Street.**

The Roosevelt Island tram.

❶ ★★ Roosevelt Island Tram and FDR Four Freedoms Park.

Roosevelt Island residents who ride the tram to and from Manhattan every day are privy to one of NYC's best-kept secrets! The view from it is awe-inspiring. Look down the East River during the 4-minute ride, and you'll see four bridges (Queensboro, Williamsburg, Manhattan, and Brooklyn). On Roosevelt Island, explore serene Franklin D. Roosevelt Four Freedoms Park. Designed by acclaimed architect Louis Kahn, the park was commissioned in 1973 by then-mayor John Lindsay. Soon after the announcement, Kahn died unexpectedly, New York went bankrupt, and the

park became a pipe dream. But the dream became a reality 39 years later when the memorial finally opened in October 2012, featuring a 1,050-pound bronze bust of Roosevelt by sculptor Jo Davidson. *Closed Tues. Tram at Second Ave. and 59th St. Fare $2.50. Subway: 4/5/6/N/R/W to 59th St.*

❷ ★★★ Free Festivals. We could write an entire book on those! The city is blessed with hundreds each year, the most iconic summer ones being **Shakespeare in the Park** (Central Park, www.publictheater.org); and **New York Philharmonic** evening concerts in parks around the city (http://nyphil.org). For a listing of current fests try NYMag.com.

❸ ★★★ New York Public Library. This magnificent Beaux Arts building has permanent and temporary exhibitions plus a nice

The New York Philharmonic playing in Central Park.

TV Tapings

It's free—but not easy—to view the tapings of such New York–based shows as *The Late Show with Stephen Colbert, The Tonight Show Starring Jimmy Fallon, Late Night with Seth Myers, Saturday Night Live,* and *The View.* The catch is ordering tickets well in advance. Check the "ticket request" section on each show's website. For a full list of all shows taping in the city, go to **NYC & Company,** the city's official tourism agency (www.nycgo.com/articles/tv-show-tapings).

gift shop in the lobby. Oh, and it's all free. *See p 8.*

④ ★★ The Museum at FIT. That would be the Fashion Institute of Technology (you've seen it on *Project Runway*). This surprisingly erudite museum never charges an entrance fee and covers topics that merge sociology and fashion (like uniforms through the ages, or how denim went from workmen's wear to high fashion). *Seventh Ave. at 27th St.* www.fitnyc.edu/museum. ☎ 212/247-4558. *Tues–Fri noon–8pm, Sat 10am–5pm.*

⑤★★ Mmuseumm. Take one abandoned elevator shaft, four documentary filmmakers/curators, and lots of dinner-plate-sized (or smaller) contemporary artifacts from around the world, and you get a fascinating, if quirky, mini-museum that explores what it means to be human today.

4 Cortlandt Alley (near White St.). www.mmuseumm.com. *Free. Thurs–Fri 6–9pm, Sat–Sun noon–6pm.*

⑥ ★★ Federal Reserve Bank of New York. With more gold than Fort Knox—$90 billion of it—you would think this urban fortress would be closed to the public. But no, it offers compelling free tours, covering the history of the Fed, its security measures, and a visit to the gold vault, 50 feet below ground. Advance reservations required. ⏱ *1 hr. 33 Liberty St. (btw. William and Nassau sts.).* www.newyorkfed.org. ☎ 212/720-6130. *Subway: 4/5 to Wall St.*

⑦ ★★ Staten Island Ferry. This free 25-minute ride takes you up close and past the Statue of Liberty and Ellis Island. *Whitehall Ferry Terminal.* www.siferry.com. ☎ 718/727-2508. ●

The Staten Island ferry.

The Metropolitan **Museum of Art**

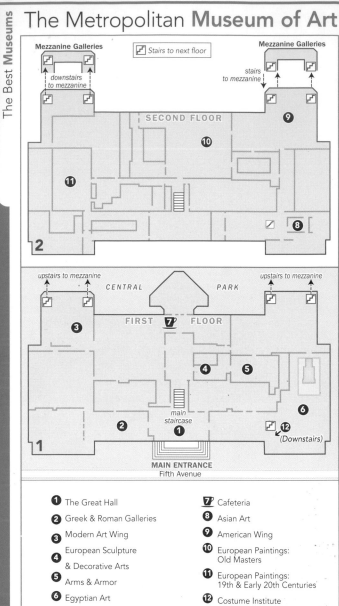

1 The Great Hall	**7** Cafeteria
2 Greek & Roman Galleries	**8** Asian Art
3 Modern Art Wing	**9** American Wing
4 European Sculpture & Decorative Arts	**10** European Paintings: Old Masters
5 Arms & Armor	**11** European Paintings: 19th & Early 20th Centuries
6 Egyptian Art	**12** Costume Institute

Previous page: The Great Hall of the Metropolitan Museum of Art.

In 1866, a group of New Yorkers decided their hometown needed a museum that would function as a living encyclopedia of world art. Today, the Metropolitan Museum of Art and the associated Met Breuer and Cloisters museums fulfill that promise with a collection of more than two million objects dating from the Paleolithic period—that is, the Stone Age—through today.

❶ The Great Hall. The main entrance to the Met makes all who enter feel like royalty. With its soaring ceilings, elegant balconies, and restrained use of Greco-Roman motifs, it's a fine example of neo-classical architecture. The massive sprays of fresh flowers have been a tradition since 1969.

❷ ★★★ Greek & Roman Galleries. Some 3,700 people per day visit these spectacular Greek and Roman galleries. The centerpiece is the **Leon Levy and Shelby White Court,** a dramatic peristyle area rich with Hellenistic and Roman art. Among its treasures is a massive statue of **Hercules** with a lion skin draped heroically over his arm. In the galleries, visitors can see **Roman frescoes** long buried under ash after a volcanic eruption; exquisite **gold serpentine armbands;** and the **"Black Bedroom,"** reputedly made for a villa built by a close friend of the Emperor Augustus.

❸ ★★★ Modern Art Wing. Head through the galleries of the Arts of Africa, Oceania, and the Americas to get to the Modern Art Wing, which is full of blockbusters. Must-sees include **Pablo Picasso's** *Gertrude Stein,* **Thomas Hart Benton's** *America Today,* and **Balthus'** *The Mountain.*

❹ ★★ European Sculpture & Decorative Arts. In these galleries, a series of period rooms include a handsome bedroom from an 18th-century **Venetian palace** and a mid-18th-century **Tapestry Room** from an English country estate. Especially astonishing is the *Studiolo* from the Ducal Palace in Gubbio, a small Renaissance study paneled in elaborate marquetry—thousands of pieces of different colored wood, giving the illusion of cabinets containing books, musical instruments, and scientific tools.

❺ ★ kids Arms & Armor. The full sets of European armor in the courtyard are dazzling, but make

Thomas Hart Benton's "America Today" in the Modern Art Wing.

Practical Matters

The Met (www.metmuseum.org; ☎ 212/535-7710; Sun–Thurs 10am–5:30pm; Fri–Sat 10am–9pm) is located at 1000 Fifth Ave. (at 82nd St.). Suggested admission is $25 adults, $17 seniors, $12 students, and free for children under 12. If you're in a rush, skip the main entrance on 82nd and enter through 81st Street. The least crowded times are Friday and Saturday nights or right at opening.

sure to pop into the smaller galleries that surround the court. Here you'll find such curiosities as ceremonial saddles carved from bone and pistols inlaid with semiprecious stones. A Turkish saber created in 1876 for the investiture of an Ottoman sultan (who had a nervous breakdown before the ceremony and was deposed) is a miracle of sparkling diamonds, smooth-as-ice jade, and rich gold.

❻ ★★★ kids Egyptian Art. The **Temple of Dendur,** built in 15 B.C. and relocated from Egypt, is arguably the most famous object at the Met. Inside, you'll find graffiti from Victorian-era travelers. For a glimpse of daily life in ancient Egypt, check out the 13 wooden models from the **tomb of Meketre,** representations of the nobleman's earthly wealth—a bakery, a dairy, a brewery, and boats--to be taken with him into the afterlife.

❼ Cafes. Year-round you can grab a good, filling lunch at one of the Met's onsite cafes—they even have kids' meals. Or, if it's a nice day, head outside the main entrance and get a snack from one of the carts ($) on the plaza. Eating a pretzel or hot dog while people-watching from the steps of the museum is a quintessential New York experience. For other dining options, *see p 111.*

❽ ★ Asian Art. The **Astor Court,** a Chinese scholar's garden based on a Ming Dynasty design, is a wonderfully serene space. The principle of yin and yang, or opposites, gives this space its sense of harmony and tranquility—that, and it's often inexplicably deserted. Also in this section: the Japanese galleries, filled with delicate scrolls, screens, kimonos, and tapestries. Our fave: the elegant **Japanese tearoom/study room.**

❾ ★★ American Wing. This airy, light-filled section of the Met is a museum inside a museum containing Hudson River School paintings that are extraordinary in their scope, from the grandeur of **Frederick Church's** *The Heart of the Andes* to the delicate and refined *Lake George* by **John Kensett.** Plenty more is recognizable here, from the iconic *Washington Crossing the Delaware* by **Emanuel Leutze** to **John Singer Sargent's** *Madame X.* The American Wing includes 25 furnished period rooms from the late 17th to the early 20th centuries, including **Frank Lloyd Wright's** suave *Living Room from the Little House.*

❿ ★★★ European Paintings: Old Masters. Where to start? These galleries hold important works from all the geniuses you studied in Art History 101 (except daVinci). Among the many

Botticelli portrait of a young man, in the European Paintings galleries.

wonders: **Rembrandt**'s *Aristotle with a Bust of Homer,* **Vermeer**'s *Young Woman with a Water Jug,* **El Greco**'s *Portrait of a Cardinal,* **Velázquez**'s *Juan de Pareja,* **Goya**'s

Don Manuel, and **Duccio**'s *Madonna and Child.*

⑪ ★★ European Paintings: 19th & Early 20th Centuries. One of the museum's most popular sections, these galleries include a good sampling of Impressionist art. Here you can compare **Gustave Courbet**'s controversial and explicitly sexual *Woman with a Parrot* with a more discreet version by **Edouard Manet.** Or take in **Paul Cézanne**'s *Still Life with Apples and Pears,* with its funky perspectives and innovative use of color, to get a feel for the radical changes in painting that developed in the 20th century.

⑫ ★★ The Costume Institute. A favorite of fashionistas, the Institute puts together blockbuster retrospectives that have, in the past, had museum-goers lining up around the block for entry.

The Cloisters & Met Breuer

That big white building on Fifth Avenue? That's just the beginning of what the Met has up its sleeve. Eight miles uptown in Fort Tryon Park, the Met off-shoot **The Cloisters** is the only museum in the U.S. wholly devoted to medieval art. It not only displays masterpieces of that era (including the ecstatically beautiful *Unicorn Tapestries)* but does so in a setting that appears airlifted, utterly intact, from a remote corner of the Pyrenees, or a castle-bound town in Bavaria. That's an illusion. The building incorporates elements from five medieval monasteries in France, Spain, and Italy. *Note:* The last stop on the M4 bus is directly in front of The Cloisters. The ride takes 1 hour. Admission is free with same-day Met sticker.

Opened in 2016, the **Met Breuer** (945 Madison Avenue btw 74th and 75th sts.) presents themed exhibitions drawn from the Met's ever-growing contemporary art collection, in the building originally created for the Whitney Museum (p 49) by Modernist master Marcel Breuer. The museum keeps almost the same hours as its mothership (it's closed Mondays) and is free with a same-day Met sticker.

Other **Must-See Museums**

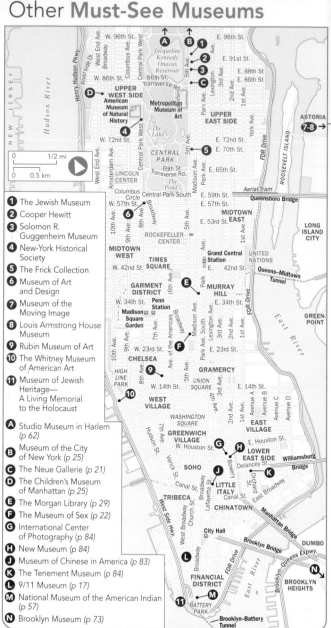

1. The Jewish Museum
2. Cooper Hewitt
3. Solomon R. Guggenheim Museum
4. New-York Historical Society
5. The Frick Collection
6. Museum of Art and Design
7. Museum of the Moving Image
8. Louis Armstrong House Museum
9. Rubin Museum of Art
10. The Whitney Museum of American Art
11. Museum of Jewish Heritage— A Living Memorial to the Holocaust

A. Studio Museum in Harlem (p 62)
B. Museum of the City of New York (p 25)
C. The Neue Gallerie (p 21)
D. The Children's Museum of Manhattan (p 25)
E. The Morgan Library (p 29)
F. The Museum of Sex (p 22)
G. International Center of Photography (p 84)
H. New Museum (p 84)
J. Museum of Chinese in America (p 83)
K. The Tenement Museum (p 84)
L. 9/11 Museum (p 17)
M. National Museum of the American Indian (p 57)
N. Brooklyn Museum (p 73)

ew cities can match New York in the breadth and depth of its museum collections. Besides the museums you'll find on various other tours in this guide, the following sites would be star attractions in any other city—but all too often fall into second place on New York City visitors' lists (and undeservedly so). *Tip:* Most museums offer free admission on the evenings they stay open late; check websites for details. Also, note that the term "suggested donation" really does mean that you can pay *whatever* you'd like for entry, without embarrassment.

The Cooper Hewitt Museum, housed in what was once Andrew Carnegie's mansion.

❶ ★★ The Jewish Museum. The "humble" goal of this institution is to cover 4000 years of Jewish history. It does so in dazzling style, with interactive panels, exquisite ceremonial objects (like menorahs and prayer shawls), other Judaica, and folk art. The only topic that doesn't get much coverage is the Holocaust—for that, go to the **Museum of Jewish Heritage** (p 49). In the basement are the best nosher in the 'hood—bagels, smoked meats and fish, borscht—at **Russ & Daughter's** restaurant. ⏱ *2 hr. 1109 Fifth Ave (at 92nd St). www.thejewishmuseum.org. ☎ 212/423-3200. Admission $15 adults, $12 seniors, $7.50 students, free to those under 18 and on Saturdays. Fri-Tues 11am–5:45 pm, Thurs 11am–8pm. Subway: 6 to 96th St.*

❷ ★★★ kids Cooper Hewitt. An off-shoot of the Smithsonian, this design museum may be one of the most cutting-edge in the country. Along with presenting expertly curated exhibits on everything from how Pixar designs films, to the work of Louis Comfort Tiffany, it encourages visitors to use a specially created "pen" to enhance appreciation of the design works on display. You can create your own website filled with objects in the museum that interest you (just press the pen to the barcode next to the item), or use the pen to activate responsive tables throughout the museum, to learn more info and ways to interact with the exhibits. ⏱ *2 hr. 2 E. 91st St. (off Fifth Ave.). www.cooper hewitt.org. ☎ 212/849-2950. Admission $18 adults, $12 seniors, $9 students, free to those under 18 and on Saturdays from 6–9pm. Sun–Fri 10am–6pm, Sat 10am–9pm. Subway: 6 to 96th St.*

❸ ★★★ **Solomon R. Guggenheim Museum.** The building alone is a masterpiece, but what's inside is often as wondrous. Along with of-the-moment themed exhibitions and installations, it offers a stroll through the canon of modern art—everything from an 1867 landscape by Camille Pissaro to important works by Picasso, Kandinsky, and Modigliani. See p 37.

❹ ★★ **New-York Historical Society.** The New-York Historical Society is a major repository of American history, culture, and art, with a special focus on New York. Where else can you find a collection that includes Tiffany lamps, vintage dollhouses, Audubon watercolors, life and death masks of prominent Americans, and even George Washington's camp bed? ⏱ 1½ hr. 2 W. 77th St. (at Central Park West). www.nyhistory.org. ☎ 212/873-3400. Admission $20 adults, $15 seniors, $12 students, $6 children 5–12, free under 5. Tues–Sat 10am–6pm (until 8pm Fri), Sun 11am–5pm. Bus: M79. Subway: 1 to 79th St.

❺ ★★★ **The Frick Collection.** Industrialist Henry Clay Frick, who controlled the steel industry in Pittsburgh in the late 19th century, began collecting art after he made his first million. Architects Carrère & Hastings built this palatial French neoclassical mansion in 1914 to house both Frick's family and his art. This living testament to New York's Gilded Age is graced with paintings from Frick's collection: works by Titian, Gainsborough, Rembrandt, Turner, Vermeer, El Greco, and Goya. A highlight is the Fragonard Room, which contains the sensual rococo series The Progress of Love. ⏱ 2 hr. 1 E. 70th St. (at Fifth Ave.). www.frick.org. ☎ 212/288-0700. Admission $22 adults, $17 seniors, $12 students. Children under 10 not admitted. Free Sundays from 11am–1pm. Tues–Sat 10am–6pm, Sun 11am–5pm. Subway: 6 to 68th St. Bus: M1/2/3/4.

❻ ★ **Museum of Art and Design.** Not as spellbinding as the Cooper-Hewitt, this towering museum (with a terrific gift shop on the ground floor) nonetheless has put on some intriguing shows over the years, such as one on designing perfumes (with sniff stations) and another on the symbolism behind the brooches Madeline Albright wore as Secretary of State. ⏱ 1 hr. 2 Columbus Circle (at 59th St.). www.madmuseum.org. ☎ 212/299-7777. Admission $16 adults, $14 seniors, $12 students, free for those under 18. Tues–Sun 10am–6pm (until 8pm Fri and Sat). Subway: A, B, C, D, 1 to 59th St./Columbus Circle.

❼ ★★ **Rubin Museum of Art.** New York must have good karma: In October 2004, it scored this

Classic movie stills at the Museum of the Moving Image.

stunning collection of Himalayan art. In the former Chelsea outpost of Barneys, the Rubin Museum features sculptures, paintings, and textiles. ⏱ *1½ hr. 150 W. 17th St. (btw. Sixth and Seventh aves.). www.rmanyc.org.* ☎ *212/620-5000. Admission $10 adults; $5 seniors, students, and artists; free for children 12 and under. Mon and Thurs 11am–5pm, Wed 11am–7pm, Fri 11am–10pm, Sat–Sun 11am–6pm. Subway: 1/9 to 18th St.*

❽ ★★★ kids Museum of the Moving Image. For sheer unadulterated fun, no museum in town that can beat this one. The first museum anywhere to look at TV, film, and video games together, it's not simply an archive of past shows. Instead, it explores the craft and technology behind these arts with imaginative interactive exhibits, art works, video sequences, and artifacts. The museum is just 2 subway stops from midtown Manhattan. ⏱ *2 hr. 36–01 35th Ave (at 37th St.), Astoria, Queens. www.movingimage. us.* ☎ *718/777-6888. Admission $15 adults, $11 seniors and students, $7 children 3–17. Wed–Thurs 10:30am–5pm, Fri 10:30am–8pm, Sat–Sun 11:30am–7pm. Subway: R to Steinway St. or Q, N to 36 Ave.*

❾ ★★ Louis Armstrong House Museum. A visit to the only home Satchmo ever owned offers a tuneful trip back in time, accompanied by witty, knowledgeable tour guides (guided tours only). You'll see his prized solid gold sink, learn about what it was like to tour with him, and get a better appreciation for the genial, incredibly brave man who changed music history. ⏱ *40 min. 34-56 107th St., Corona, Queens. www.louis armstronghouse.org.* ☎ *718/478-8274. Admission: $10 adults, $7 seniors, students, and children. Tues–Fri 10am–5pm, Sat–Sun noon–5pm. Subway: 7 to 103 St.-Corona Pl.*

❿ ★★★ The Whitney Museum of American Art. Reborn in 2016, this mecca of American art is now located in the hippest neighborhood in Manhattan, right at the foot of the High Line (p 104). Which is appropriate, as the museum—originally built in 1931 around Gertrude Vanderbilt Whitney's collection of 20th-century art (including still-displayed works by Edward Hopper, Jasper Johns, and Georgia O'Keefe)—has become a major player in the contemporary art scene, much of which is centered in the nearby Chelsea galleries (see p 64). ⏱ *2 hr. 99 Gansevoort St. (btw. Washington St. and Tenth Ave.). http://whitney.org.* ☎ *800/WHITNEY (944-8639). Admission $25 adults, $18 seniors and students, free for children 18 and under and Fri 7–10pm. Online discount for those who purchase in advance. Wed–Thurs and Sun 10:30am–6pm, Fri–Sat 10:30am–10pm. Subway: 6 to 77th St.*

⓫ ★ Museum of Jewish Heritage—A Living Memorial to the Holocaust. Dedicated to teaching people of all backgrounds about 20th-century Jewish life, this award-winning museum was designed in a six-sided shape to symbolize the Star of David and to honor the six million Jews who died in the Holocaust. Inside are photos, artifacts, and moving accounts from survivors. A second-story stone garden—where each of the hollowed-out boulders has a tree growing out of it—overlooks New York Harbor. ⏱ *2 hr. 36 Battery Place. www.mjhnyc.org.* ☎ *646/437-4200. Admission $12 adults, $10 seniors, $7 students, free for children 12 and under. Sun–Tues and Thurs 10am–5:45pm, Wed 10am–8pm, Fri 10am–5pm, eves of Jewish holidays 10am–3pm. Subway: 4/5 to Bowling Green; 1 to South Ferry.*

The American Museum of **Natural History**

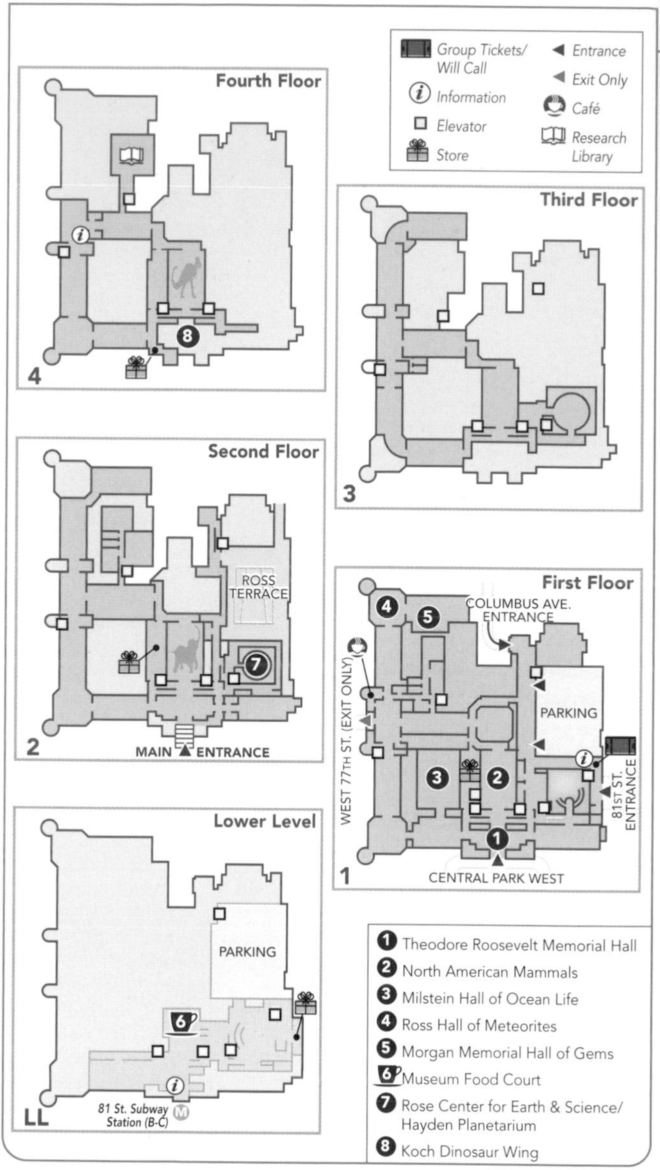
Group Tickets/ Will Call
Information
Elevator
Store
Entrance
Exit Only
Café
Research Library
Fourth Floor
4
Third Floor
3
Second Floor
ROSS TERRACE
MAIN ENTRANCE
2
First Floor
COLUMBUS AVE. ENTRANCE
PARKING
WEST 77TH ST. (EXIT ONLY)
81ST ST. ENTRANCE
CENTRAL PARK WEST
1
Lower Level
PARKING
81 St. Subway Station (B-C)
LL
1 Theodore Roosevelt Memorial Hall
2 North American Mammals
3 Milstein Hall of Ocean Life
4 Ross Hall of Meteorites
5 Morgan Memorial Hall of Gems
6 Museum Food Court
7 Rose Center for Earth & Science/ Hayden Planetarium
8 Koch Dinosaur Wing

It's got dinosaurs, giant sapphires, and towering totem poles—and that's just for starters. The American Museum of Natural History has one of the most diverse and thrilling collections in the world—four floors of natural wonders and cultural artifacts for the intrepid explorer in all of us. It's delicious fun for every age.

❶ ★★ **Theodore Roosevelt Memorial Hall.** The sight of a giant *Barosaurus* fossil in this soaring entrance rotunda provides a smashing opening to the rest of your visit.

❷ ★★ **North American Mammals.** One of the museum's popular "Habitat Group Dioramas," where skillfully mounted animals are shown in lifelike reproductions of their natural habitats. In one diorama, an Alaskan brown bear, the world's largest living land carnivore, rears up on its hind legs.

❸ ★★ **Milstein Hall of Ocean Life.** This vast first-floor room explores life in the deep blue sea, with lighted fish dioramas and a spectacular replica of a giant blue whale overhead.

❹ ★★ **Ross Hall of Meteorites.** On display is a 34-ton meteorite, said to be merely a fragment of a massive meteorite that scientists estimate weighed around 200 tons.

❺ ★ **Morgan Memorial Hall of Gems.** This collection of precious gems includes the biggest sapphire ever found, the 563-carat Star of India.

❻ **Museum Food Court.** Sustenance for the whole family, including barbecue, paninis, and sandwiches. *Lower level. $–$$.*

❼ ★★★ **Rose Center for Earth & Space/Hayden Planetarium.** A sphere inside a seven-story glass cube holds the Hayden Planetarium, where you can take a virtual ride through the Milky Way. Prepare to be blown away by the planetarium **Space Show,** narrated by Neil deGrasse Tyson. Buy tickets in advance for the Space Show to guarantee admission (they're available online).

❽ ★★★ **Koch Dinosaur Wing.** The fourth floor contains the largest collection of real dinosaur fossils in the world. Among the treasures is the *Tyrannosaurus rex*, with 6-inch-long teeth, and the first *Velociraptor* skull ever found.

Practical Matters

The AMNH (www.amnh.org; ☎ 212/769-5100; daily 10am–5:45pm) is on Central Park West (btw. 77th and 81st sts.). Admission (includes entrance to Rose Center) is $22 adults, $17 seniors and students, $12 children 2 to 12; museum admission plus Space Show is $27 adults, $22 seniors and students, $16 children 2 to 12. You'll need about 4 hours to see the whole thing. Buy tickets in advance for specific IMAX shows or special exhibitions. Subway: B, C to 81st St.

The Museum of **Modern Art**

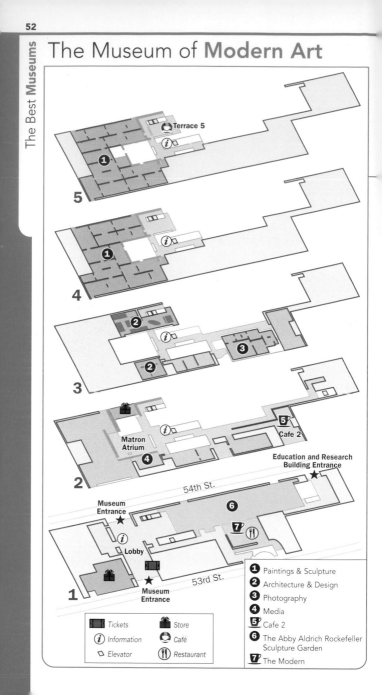

Terrace 5

1

5

1

4

2

2

3

3

Matron
Atrium

Cafe 2

5

4

Education and Research
Building Entrance

54th St.

6

Museum
Entrance

7

Lobby

53rd St.

Museum
Entrance

Tickets

Store

(i) Information

Café

Elevator

Restaurant

1 Paintings & Sculpture
2 Architecture & Design
3 Photography
4 Media
5 Cafe 2
6 The Abby Aldrich Rockefeller
   Sculpture Garden
7 The Modern

For art that's termed "modern"—the stuff that was created from the 1860's to the 1970's—this museum is without peer. For contemporary art, it now has important rivals (we're looking at you, Whitney). Still, the strength of its collection makes it an essential stop on any New York jaunt. A 2010 remodeling of the building by Yoshio Taniguchi created a wonderland of space and light, with open rooms, high ceilings, and gardens. It's a beautiful work of architecture that complements the art within—a vast repository of paintings, drawings, photographs, architectural models, film, video and modern furniture.

Studying Barnett Newman's Vir Heroicus Sublimis at the Museum of Modern Art.

❶ ★★★ Painting & Sculpture.
Start your tour at the top: on the fifth floor for works from the 1880's–1940's, fourth floor for 1940's–1970's. Among the museum treasures are **Vincent van Gogh**'s *The Starry Night*, **Andrew Wyeth**'s *Christina's World*, **Picasso**'s *Les Demoiselles d'Avignon*, and **Henri Rousseau**'s *The Sleeping Gypsy*. Look for celebrated works by Henri Matisse, Paul Gauguin, Marc

Chagall, Paul Cézanne, Edward Hopper, René Magritte, Willem de Kooning, Mark Rothko, Frank Stella, and Jackson Pollock.

❷ ★★★ Architecture & Design. The third floor contains some 28,000 works that, perhaps more than any other collection, reflect the form-follows-function dynamism of the modern era. Here are Eames chairs, Frank Lloyd Wright windows, a 1908 Peter

Practical Matters

The MoMA (www.moma.org; ☎ 212/708-9400; Sat–Thurs 10:30am–5:30pm, Fri 10:30am–8pm) is at 11 W. 53rd St. (btw. Fifth and Sixth aves.). Admission is $25 adults, $18 seniors, $14 students, and free for kids 16 and under and on Fridays from 4 to 8pm. You'll need 3 hours to do it justice. Subway: E,M to Fifth Ave/53rd St.

Behrens fan, and even elegantly designed ball bearings.

3 ★★ Photography.

MoMA started collecting photographs in 1930, well before most people considered photography an art form. The stunning collection on the third floor holds important works by Walker Evans, Man Ray, and Cindy Sherman, as well as mid-19th-century albumen silver prints from glass-plate negatives.

Travel Tip

MoMA's museum-wide Wi-Fi allows visitors to access to excellent audio tours. Content is available in specialized versions for children, teenagers, and the visually impaired.

4 ★ Media.

This collection on the second floor covers some 50 years of works in media, from moving-image installations and short films to pieces that combine avant-garde performance art and video.

5 ★ Cafe 2.

Forget the museum cafes of old, with rubbery food and harsh lighting. This museum cafe has a soft wood-and-gold shimmer and serves handmade pastas, artisanal cheeses, seasonal soups, paninis, and decent wines. *2nd floor. $–$$.*

6 ★★ Abby Aldrich Rockefeller Sculpture Garden.

This landscaped outdoor space holds such gems as **Picasso**'s whimsical *She-Goat* (1950) and **Alberto Giacometti**'s long, lean *Tall Figure III* (1960) as well as installations by contemporary artists such as **Richard Serra**.

7 ★★ The Modern.

Whether you're here for lunch, dinner, or a cocktail, this is a destination in itself. It's sleek and fabulous, with big glass windows overlooking the sculpture garden and superb food. *1st floor. www.themodernnyc.com. ☎ 212/333-1220. $$$. ●*

P.S. 1 Contemporary Art Center

If you're interested in new work that's thrillingly cutting-edge, this MoMA affiliate is worth the trip—one stop outside Manhattan in Queens. Originally a public school, **P.S. 1** (22–25 Jackson Ave. at 46th Ave., Long Island City; www.ps1.org; ☎ 718/784-2084; Thurs–Mon noon–6pm) is one of the country's largest nonprofit art institutions, exhibiting contemporary art from America and abroad. The array of works includes large-scale exhibitions by such artists as Mark Leckey and virtual reality pieces by Bjork. Almost as enticing as the art is the innovative food served at the museum's restaurant, **M. Wells Dinette** (☎ 718/786-1800; $$). Museum admission is $10 adults, $5 seniors and students, free for children under 16. Subway: E or M to 23rd Street/Ely Avenue, 7 train to 45th Rd./Court House Square.

4 The Best Neighborhood Walks

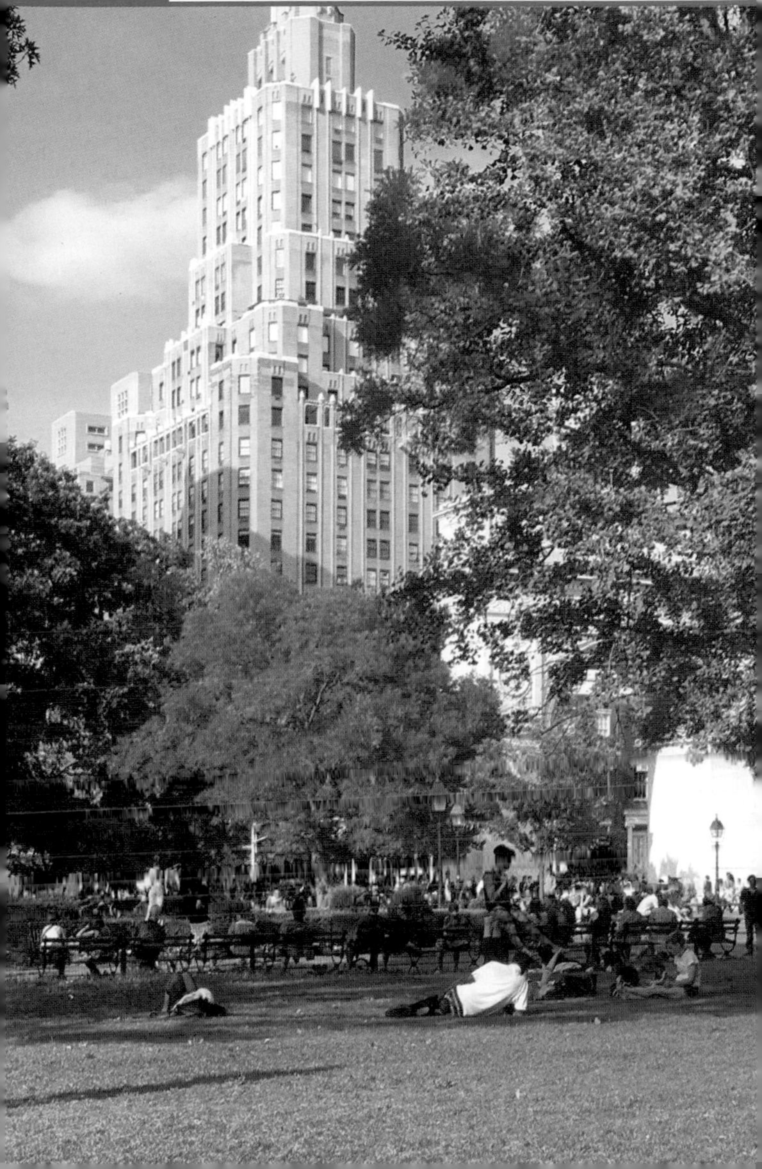

The Financial District

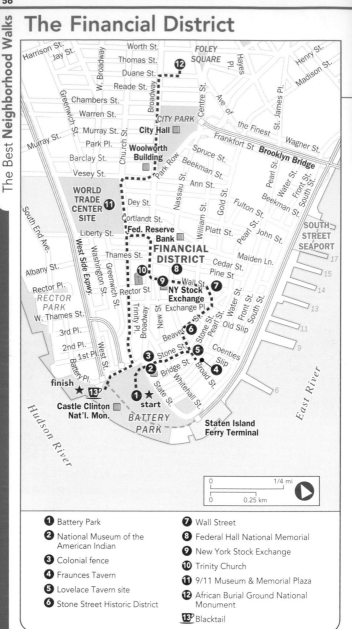

- **1** Battery Park
- **2** National Museum of the American Indian
- **3** Colonial fence
- **4** Fraunces Tavern
- **5** Lovelace Tavern site
- **6** Stone Street Historic District
- **7** Wall Street
- **8** Federal Hall National Memorial
- **9** New York Stock Exchange
- **10** Trinity Church
- **11** 9/11 Museum & Memorial Plaza
- **12** African Burial Ground National Monument
- **13** Blacktail

Previous page: Hanging out in Washington Square Park.

The southern tip of Manhattan is where the city as we know it began. You'll explore 17th-century cobblestone alleyways, the seaport where 18th-century commerce helped build the city, historic landmarks of the American Revolution, and the canyons of Wall Street, constructed in outsize Deco style in the early 20th century. START: **Subway 4/5 to Bowling Green or 1 to South Ferry.**

1 ★★ Battery Park. Look out at the river: It's the reason this great city was built. When Henry Hudson sailed up it in 1609, mistakenly thinking he'd find Asia at its mouth, little did he know he was setting into motion a chain of events that would still be shaping lives over 400 years later. Hudson's reports about the trading possibilities of the area (particularly for valuable animal pelts), plus his amazement at the great natural harbor, spurred the Dutch to create settlements. They guessed—rightly, it turned out—that the harbor of New York would be the linchpin connecting Europe (via the Atlantic Ocean) with the interior of this vast and wealthy continent (via the Hudson River). Gaze across the harbor to see the **Statue of Liberty.** (See p 15 for more.)

The National Museum of the American Indian is located within the historic Alexander Hamilton U.S. Custom House.

2 ★★★ National Museum of the American Indian. Once you leave the park, head to this landmark, though you don't have to go inside (an off-shoot of the Smithsonian, with only touring shows, the exhibits can be hit-or-miss). Instead study the façade: This was once the Alexander Hamilton U.S. Custom House. Before 1913, when personal income tax was instituted, the federal government's revenue came almost entirely from customs on goods imported into the States. And a full 75% of this revenue came from the Port of New York, where it was processed in this appropriately grand Beaux Arts colossus, completed in 1907. Daniel Chester French (who did the moving sculpture of Lincoln at the Lincoln Memorial in Washington, D.C.) created the sculptures out front; his choice of symbols could be used as a treatise on the prejudices of Victorian America. The four seated women represent the four "great" continents of the world. From left to right as you look at them, they are Asia (soon in meditation), the Americas (South America barely present, is the Aztec-like structure that North America has her foot on); Europe, and a slumbering Africa. In the footstep of this building stood the Dutch settlers' original fort. *1 Bowling Green. www.nmai.si.edu.* ☎ *212/514-3700. Free admission. Daily 10am–5pm.*

3 ★★ Colonial Fence. The fence that rings Bowling Green Park is the original, one of the few

Fraunces Tavern.

Colonial structures of any sort left in Manhattan. When it was first erected, its spokes had royal crowns at their tips. These were destroyed by colonists on July 9, 1776, when the Declaration of Independence was first read aloud in this very park.

❹ ★ Fraunces Tavern Museum. It was on this site that George Washington bade farewell to his officers at the end of the American Revolution. The museum here (in the 1907 replica of the original 1717 tavern) has period rooms, art, and artifacts (including a lock of Washington's hair and one of his false teeth). In 1975, an extremist Puerto Rican nationalist group bombed the tavern, killing four. ⏱ *45 min. 54 Pearl St. (near Broad St.). www.frauncestavern museum.org.* ☎ *212/425-1778. Admission $7 adults, $4 seniors, students, and children 6–18, free for children 5 and under. Mon–Fri noon– 5pm, Sat–Sun 11am–5pm.*

❺ ★ Lovelace Tavern Site. Little is left of 17th-century New York,

but an excavation in 1979 led to the discovery of the foundation of Lovelace Tavern, built in 1670. In an ingenious move, the underground excavation was left in place—as was an early-18th-century cistern— and the sidewalk above it was replaced with Plexiglas, so that anyone walking by can look down and see the old foundation and artifacts. *Pearl St. at Coenties Alley.*

❻ ★★ Stone Street Historic District. This 17th-century cobblestone alley has become a mini–dining-and-drinking enclave, with outdoor restaurants and bars. *See p 33.*

❼ ★★★ Wall Street. The street synonymous with high finance began, literally, in 1653 as a 12-foot-high (3.6m) wooden palisade built by the Dutch to keep out the British. (Whoops! They eventually invaded by sea.) Today, it's home to some of the city's most magnificent architecture, skyscraping Jazz Age marvels made all the more impressive by the narrowness of the streets. Check out the BNY Mellon Building, **1 Wall St.,** a tiered limestone Art Deco gem built in 1931. In 1920, a bomb exploded in front of **23 Wall St.**— then the headquarters of J. P. Morgan—killing 38 people and injuring 400; no one knows who set it, but you can still see the pock marks it caused in the wall of the building. Farther down the block at **40 Wall St.** is a building that was for a nanosecond the tallest in the world; the 1930 Deco beauty was soon overtaken in height by the Chrysler Building (p 34). *Wall St. (btw. Broadway and FDR Dr.).*

❽ ★ Federal Hall National Memorial. This majestic 1842 structure is one of Wall Street's most recognizable monuments. On this site, before the Revolutionary War, the Stamp Act Congress met to rail against "taxation without representation." Later, the First Congress wrote the Bill of Rights here, and out in front George Washington was inaugurated, on April 30, 1789 (right where his statue stands today).Head inside to see the magnificent rotunda, one of the loveliest public spaces in the city. The capital moved to Philadelphia in 1790, and the original Federal Hall was torn down in 1812. ⓘ 15 min. 26 Wall St. (btw. Nassau and William sts.). www.nps.gov/feha. ☎ 212/825-6888. Free admission. Mon–Sat 9am–5pm.

⑨ ★ New York Stock Exchange. The world's largest securities exchange, the NYSE came into being in 1792, when merchants met daily under a nearby buttonwood tree to trade U.S.

Statue of George Washington outside the Federal Hall National Memorial.

bonds that had funded the Revolutionary War. In 1903, traders moved into this Beaux Arts building designed by George Post. Surrounded by heavy security the NYSE is not open to the public. *At Broad and Wall sts.*

⑩ ★★ Trinity Church. Alexander Hamilton is buried in the church's south cemetery. The original building was erected in 1698, although the present structure dates from 1846. *See p 16.*

⑪ ★★★ 9/11 Museum and Memorial Plaza. One of the nation's greatest history museums and most sobering memorials. A must-see. *See p 17 for more.*

⑫ African Burial Ground National Monument. During construction of an office tower here in 1991, masses of human remains were unearthed. Research revealed that the area was a burial ground for slaves and freedmen. The site was designated a National Historic Landmark, and in 2007 a granite memorial was built to pay tribute to the estimated 15,000 Africans and African Americans who were buried here. *Duane and Elk sts. Visitor center at 290 Broadway. www.nps.gov/ afbg.* ☎ 212/637-2019. *Daily 9am– 5pm (till 4pm in winter); visitor center and indoor exhibitions Tues–Sat 10am–4pm. Free admission.*

⑬ ★★ Blacktail. Cap off a long day of sightseeing with a daiquiri and a snack (the pressed sandwiches are the bomb) at this ritzy, 1930's-themed bar/restaurant. *On Pier A (Battery Park, near Little West St.). www.blacktailnyc.com.* ☎ 212/785-0153. $–$$$.

Historic **Harlem**

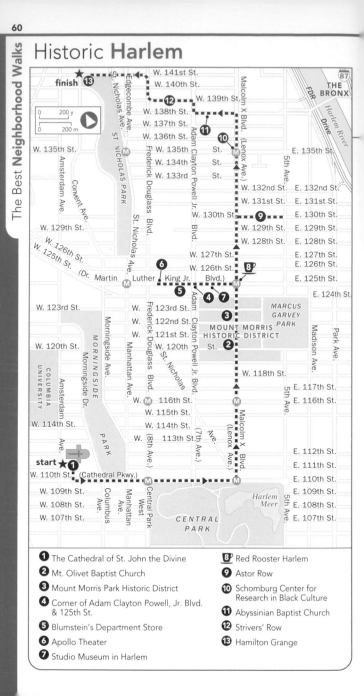

1. The Cathedral of St. John the Divine
2. Mt. Olivet Baptist Church
3. Mount Morris Park Historic District
4. Corner of Adam Clayton Powell, Jr. Blvd. & 125th St.
5. Blumstein's Department Store
6. Apollo Theater
7. Studio Museum in Harlem
8. Red Rooster Harlem
9. Astor Row
10. Schomburg Center for Research in Black Culture
11. Abyssinian Baptist Church
12. Strivers' Row
13. Hamilton Grange

It wasn't until the mid–19th century that Nieuw Amsterdam and Nieuw Haarlem—the two towns the Dutch founded on the isle of Manhattan—became one. Claimed by a number of different immigrant communities over the years, the neighborhood became renowned in the 1920's (the "Harlem Renaissance") as a mecca of black culture, and still retains that identity today. START: **Subway 1 to 110th St.**

The elaborate front facade of St. John the Divine.

❶ ★★★ The Cathedral of St. John the Divine. The largest cathedral in the world is *not* St. Peter's in Rome (which is technically a basilica). It's this Episcopalian house of worship. Construction on it began in 1892, but the building is not expected to be completed for another 100 years. That's because the 121,000-square-foot structure, a blend of Romanesque and Gothic elements, is being built without steel, in the classic Gothic manner (a fascinating process for visitors to watch. There's still much work to be done but what's in place—and there's a lot—is quite beautiful, especially the Rose Window in the apse, the largest in North America. ⏱ *45 min. 1047 Amsterdam Ave. (btw. 111th and 112th sts.). www. stjohndivine.org.* ☎ *212/316-7490. Public tours $12 adults, $10 students and seniors. Daily 7:30am–6pm. Subway: 1/9 to 110th St.*

❷ ★ Mt. Olivet Baptist Church. Look closely and you'll notice something one doesn't usually see on the facade of a church: Stars of David. This church epitomizes the neighborhood's demographic transformation from Irish immigrants, to those from Eastern Europe, to blacks escaping the American south. It was built (in 1907) to be the area's first synagogue, by the first Jewish architect licensed in New York State. He based its design on that of the Second Temple in Jerusalem, which had just been excavated, making worldwide headlines. *120th St. and Malcolm X Blvd.*

❸ Mount Morris Park Historic District. This impressively preserved collection of handsome 19th- and 20th-century brownstones features various styles, from Romanesque Revival to Queen Anne. *Bounded by 119th St., 124th St., Adam Clayton Powell Blvd. and Mount Morris Park West.*

❹ ★★ Corner of Adam Clayton Powell, Jr. Blvd and 125th St. Look first at the statue of Adam Clayton Powell, Jr., Harlem's first African American congressman. Where it stands is the spot where Malcolm X spent many long hours giving speeches on behalf of the Nation of Islam. Now, look across the street at the tall white building with geometric patterns, the former Hotel Theresa. In 1960, a young Fidel Castro was asked to speak at the United Nations and stayed here. Repeated clashes between pro- and anti-Castro forces outside the hotel kept the 258-police contingent assigned to Castro busy. On his second day at the Theresa, Nikita Khrushchev came to visit, and his police contingent plus Castro's created the greatest show of force Harlem's ever witnessed. Four years later, when Malcolm X broke with the Nation of Islam to found his own Organization of Afro-American Unity he took offices in the Teresa. When he was assassinated in 1965, this is where massive crowds gathered to mourn.

⑤ Blumstein's Department Store. Now just a faded facade, this was once the neighborhood's most fashionable store and the site of a paradigm-shifting social crusade. In 1934, the Urban League began a campaign to boycott and picket the store until it changed its hiring practices. Up until that point, though the vast majority of its clientele was African American, Blumstein's refused to hire any black store clerks. The action lasted 2 months, until Blumstein's finally relented. Dr. Martin Luther King, Jr. often spoke of this strike as an example of the power of non-violent protest. Many years after the boycott, a would-be assassin stabbed King while he was doing a book-signing at the store. He survived, but spent weeks in the hospital recuperating. *230 W. 125th St. (Frederick Douglass Blvd.).*

⑥ ★★★ Apollo Theater. This legendary venue has featured them all—Count Basie, Billie Holiday, Louis Armstrong, Duke Ellington, Marvin Gaye, Aretha Franklin, and more. "Amateur Night at the Apollo" launched the careers of Ella Fitzgerald, James Brown, Lauryn Hill, and the Jackson 5—and it's still going strong. *253 W. 125th St. (Frederick Douglass Blvd.). www. apollotheater.org.* ☎ *212/531-5300. Amateur Night tickets $19–$40.*

⑦ ★ Studio Museum in Harlem. Since 1968, the SMH has been devoted to collecting, preserving, and promoting 19th- and 20th-century African-American art as well as traditional African art and artifacts. ⏱ *1 hr. 144 W. 125th St. (btw. Lenox Ave. and Adam Clayton Powell, Jr., Blvd.). www.studio museum.org.* ☎ *212/864-4500. Admission $7 adults, $3 seniors and students, free for children 12 and under (free admission for all Sun). Thurs–Fri noon–9pm, Sat 10am–6pm, Sun noon–6pm. Subway: 2/3/A/B/ C/D to 125th St.*

Statue of Adam Clayton Powell Jr. on 125th Street.

Randy Weston performs on stage as the Jazz Foundation of America celebrates A Great Night in Harlem *at The Apollo Theater*

8 ★★ **Red Rooster Harlem.** For a taste of modern Harlem, hit up chef Marcus Samuelsson's cheerful comfort food hot spot. Don't miss the shrimp and grits. *310 Lenox Ave. (btw. 125th and 126th sts.). www.redroosterharlem.com.* ☎ *212/792-9001. $$–$$$.*

9 **Astor Row.** Built by the Astor family in the 1880s, this 28-home row of red-brick town houses might remind you of a sleepy block in Savannah, Georgia, thanks to the front yards and porches (a rarity in NYC). ⏲ *20 min. 130th St. (btw. Fifth and Lenox aves.). Subway: 2/3 to 135th St.*

10 ★★★ **Schomburg Center for Research in Black Culture.** This national research library has more than five million items documenting the experiences of African Americans, including manuscripts, rare books, moving images, artifacts and more. ⏲ *45 min. 515 Malcolm X Blvd. (btw. 135th and 136th sts.). www.nypl.org.* ☎ *212/491-2200. Free admission. Mon–Wed noon–8pm, Thurs–Fri 11am–6pm, Sat 10am–5pm. Subway: 2/3 to 135th St.*

11 **Abyssinian Baptist Church.** This Baptist church's congregation first gathered downtown in 1808, when a group of African Americans and Ethiopians withdrew from the First Baptist Church to protest its segregated seating. The congregation grew here in 1922 under the leadership of activist Adam Clayton Powell, Sr. You can join Sunday services at 9am and 11am. ⏲ *20 min. 132 W. Odell Clark Place (formerly 138th St., btw. Malcolm X Blvd. and Adam Clayton Powell, Jr., Blvd.). www.abyssinian.org.* ☎ *212/862-7474. Subway: 2/3 to 135th St.*

12 ★ **Strivers' Row.** Hardly a brick has changed on these McKim, Mead & White neo–Italian Renaissance town houses since they were built in 1890. Once the original owners had moved out, the brownstones attracted the cream of the new Harlem, including such "strivers" as composers Eubie Blake and W. C. Handy. *W. 139th St. (btw Adam Clayton Powell, Jr., and Frederick Douglass blvds.).*

13 ★ **Hamilton Grange.** The only house founding father Alexander Hamilton ever owned (built in 1802), it's a poignant visit for fans of the musical, despite the fact that almost none of the original furnishings survive. Ranger-guided tours are informative. ⏲ *1 hr. 414 W. 141st St. (btw. St. Nicholas and Convent aves). www.nps.gov/hagr.* ☎ *212/825-6990. Free admission. Daily 9am–5pm.*

Chelsea's Art & Architecture

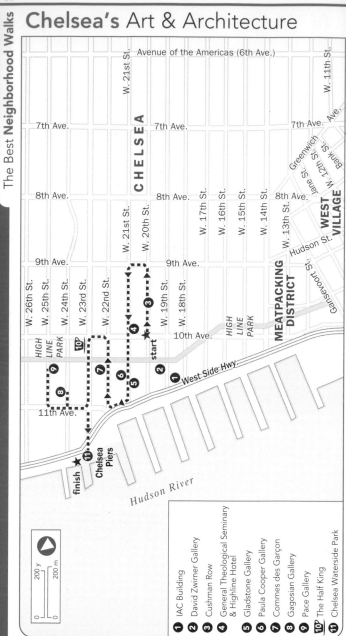

1. IAC Building
2. David Zwirner Gallery
3. Cushman Row
4. General Theological Seminary & Highline Hotel
5. Gladstone Gallery
6. Paula Cooper Gallery
7. Commes des Garçon
8. Gagosian Gallery
9. Pace Gallery
10. The Half King
11. Chelsea Waterside Park

NYC has more galleries than any other city in the world, making it the de facto contemporary art capital. The densest concentration of them is in Chelsea, though rising rents have pushed some to the Lower East Side (p 80) and to Williamsburg, Brooklyn. Spending an afternoon wandering from one to the next is a good way to get a handle on the cultural zeitgeist of today. We've listed a few of the biggest players in this tour, but if you see a gallery that intrigues you, head in—you'll likely be rewarded. START: **Subway C, E to 23rd St.**

❶ ★★★ **IAC Building.** We'll start with the art of architecture, which took a big leap forward in 2004 when this billowy building (at 555 W. 18th. St.) made its debut. It's the first Frank Gehry structure to have an all glass exterior, and it's a very special glass, warped into curves and covered with a dotted insulation that makes the building energy efficient. Across the street is French architect Jean Nouvel's equally whiz-bang building (at 100 Eleventh Ave.) with its pixilated curtain wall inspired by the eyes of insects (lots of panes of glass, each of a different diameter and tilt).

❷ ★★★ **David Zwirner Gallery.** Zwirner's majestic, two-floor gallery shows artists as varied as cartoonist R. Crumb and minimalist John McCracken. *537 W. 20th St. (btw. Tenth and Eleventh aves.). www.davidzwirner.com.* ☎ *212/517-8677. Tues–Sat 10am–6pm.*

High Line Hotel.

❸ ★ **Cushman Row.** In the late 1830s, much of Chelsea's real estate was developed by merchant Don Alonzo Cushman. His little empire included these 1840 Greek

A Day of Play at Chelsea Piers

All this art and history got your blood going? It may be time to hit the links. At the massive Chelsea Piers sports complex, you can drive golf balls out over the Hudson River (caught by a giant net, of course) to your heart's content. The complex also has a bowling alley, batting cages, sundecks, an ice rink, and basketball courts. *23rd St. and Hudson River. www.chelseapiers.com.* ☎ *212/336-6400. Oct–Mar daily 6:30am–11pm; Apr–Sept daily 6:30am–midnight. Subway: C/E to 23rd St.*

The Gladstone Gallery.

Revival houses, considered to be among the best of that style in the nation. *406–418 W. 20th St. (btw. Ninth and Tenth aves.).*

❹ ★★ General Theological Seminary and High Line Hotel. Filling up an entire city block, this historic property holds both the hip High Line Hotel (p 159) and the General Theological Seminary of the Episcopal Church, the denomination's oldest seminary, founded in 1817. It's a private working seminary, but visitors can tour the grassy grounds (the land was donated by

Clement Clarke Moore, author of *'Twas the Night Before Christmas*), the stunning 1888 **Chapel of the Good Shepherd,** and the exquisite vaulted **Refectory** in Hoffman Hall. *440 W. 21st St. (btw. Ninth and Tenth aves.). www.gts.edu. ☎ 212/ 243-5150. Mon–Fri 10am–3pm.*

❺ ★★ Gladstone Gallery. Gladstone's sizable roster of American and European artists includes such famous names as German artist Rosemarie Trockel and Keith Haring. A second location is at 515 W. 24th St. *530 W. 21st St. (btw. Tenth and Eleventh aves.). www. gladstonegallery.com. ☎ 212/206-7606. Tues–Sat 10am–6pm.*

❻ ★ Paula Cooper Gallery. Works by such major artists as Donald Judd, Sol Lewitt, and Jennifer Bartlett can be found in this loftlike space. *534 W. 21st St. (btw. Tenth and Eleventh aves.). www.paula coopergallery.com. ☎ 212/255-1105. Tues–Sat 10am–6pm.*

❼ ★★ Commes des Garçons. This shop has no number, no signage—just look for the egg-shaped "spaceship" entryway cut

The Paula Cooper Gallery.

The futuristic entryway of the Commes des Garçon clothing store.

into a red-brick facade. Then pass through the silver aluminum tunnel into a crisp white labyrinth full of designer Rei Kawakubo's ultraexpensive clothing. *520 W. 22nd St. (btw. Tenth and Eleventh aves.).* ☎ *212/604 9200.*

⑧ ★★★ Gagosian Gallery. Most of Chelsea's galleries aren't large enough to hold more than one major exhibition at a time, but the white high-ceilinged rooms in the Gagosian feel like a mini-museum. The gallery pulls off major feats like 2016's acclaimed show of Richard Serra's monolithic steel slabs. *555 W. 24th St. (btw. Tenth and Eleventh aves.). www.gagosian. com* ☎ *212/741 1111. Mon–Sat 10am–6pm.*

⑨ ★ The Pace Gallery. One of the world's best-known galleries, it displays only major artists, both living and dead—from Chuck Close to Mark Rothko. Pace has another Chelsea outpost at 534 W. 25th St. *508–510 W. 25th St. (btw. Tenth and Eleventh aves.). www.thepacegallery. com.* ☎ *212/989-4258. Tues–Sat 10am–6pm.*

⑩ ★ The Half King. A pub with a literary pedigree—it's owned by Sebastian Junger (author of The Perfect Storm)—so you're likely to get an author's reading with your Guinness, your burger, mac 'n' cheese, or potpie (if you come in the early evening). The food is good, but the conversations between regulars and visitors at the bar is even better. *505 W. 23rd St. (at Tenth Ave.). www.thehalfking. com.* ☎ *212/462-4300. $–$$.*

⑪ Chelsea Waterside Park. Walk off the pub grub: Next door to the Chelsea Piers sports complex, Pier 62 has been handsomely landscaped and has a California-style skatepark and a sweet little carousel with hand-carved Hudson Valley woodland creatures. Grounds curve down to the river, where you can sit and take in the glittering riverscape *Across Eleventh Ave. at 23rd St. and West Side Hwy.*

Practical Matters

Most galleries in Chelsea are closed on Sundays and Mondays, have special summer hours, and close temporarily (and randomly) for exhibition changes. Almost all are free to visit.

Greenwich Village

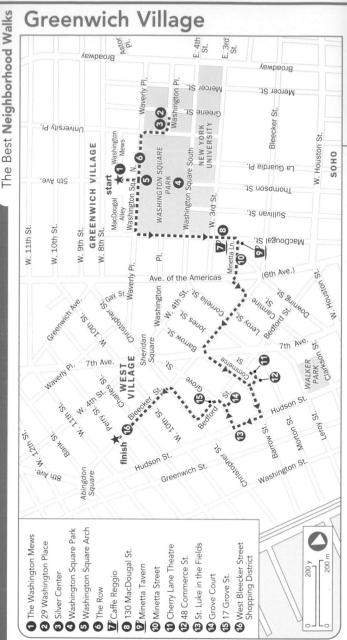

1 The Washington Mews
2 29 Washington Place
3 Silver Center
4 Washington Square Park
5 Washington Square Arch
6 The Row
7 Caffe Reggio
8 130 MacDougal St.
9 Minetta Tavern
10 Minetta Street
11 Cherry Lane Theatre
12 48 Commerce St.
13 St. Luke in the Fields
14 Grove Court
15 17 Grove St.
16 West Bleecker Street
   Shopping District

Greenwich Village started as its own village, a place where the well-to-do fled on a yearly basis to escape the plagues of Nieuw Amsterdam and New York (yellow fever, primarily). Building began in earnest in the 1820s in this genteel "suburb". When the hoi polloi moved in, the blue bloods did the 19th-century version of urban flight and moved a mile uptown. Swank townhouses were subdivided into cheap apartments and boarding houses, and the neighborhood became one of factories and immigrants, and later artists. It's a wealthy area today, but retains its artistic spirit. START: Subway N/R to 8th St.

❶ ★ The Washington Mews.

Visitors who stumble upon this cobbled alleyway discover a living slice of old New York. The north side of the mews consists of original 19th-century stables converted into stuccoed houses. *Enter at University Place or Fifth Ave. (btw. 8th St. and Waverly Place).*

❷ ★★ 29 Washington Place.

On March 25, 1911, a horrific tragedy here reshaped the history of the American labor movement. Some 600 young women, Jewish and Italian immigrants between the ages of 13 and 23, were laboring inside what was the Triangle Shirtwaist factory when a fire started. Because the owners had locked the women inside (to prevent theft, they later said), many couldn't escape. Girls started jumping to their deaths in front of horrified passersby; in all 146 were killed. As a result, New York's labor code was re-written to become the most stringent in the nation, and the Ladies Garment Workers Union grew in strength. The building, now part of New York University, is the original one. *At the NW corner of Washington Pl. and Greene St.*

❸ Silver Center. Dash-dot-dot-dash—this is the birthplace of the telegraph. In 1836, New York University painting professor Samuel Morse formulated the rudiments of the telegraphic alphabet (Morse Code). In 1837, using 1,700 feet of copper wire (which he coiled around his room), he sent the first wire dispatches from one end to the other. Witnessing the experiment, student William Vail, scion of a wealthy iron-making family, convinced his father to invest in the new technology—and together they created a revolution in communications. *Corner of Washington Square E. and Washington Square N.*

❹ ★★★ Washington Square Park. Originally drained marshland given to freed slaves to farm in 1641 (they had to hand over much of their harvest each year), in 1797 this then-remote area became a potters field where some 20,000 souls were buried (many in 1798, when yellow fever wiped out 5% of the city's population). In 1826 it

Playing chess in Washington Square Park.

became a military parade ground, and tales abounded of marching soldiers crunching their boots down on shroud-covered skeletons; there were also public hangings from the massive elm still standing on its northwest corner. In 1850, when Greenwich Village became fashionable, it was re-landscaped as a formal park. By the 1960's it had become a hang-out spot for students, hippies, artists, and musicians performing for pocket change—a tradition that continues today. *Bordered by University and Waverly places and W. 4th and Macdougal sts.*

⑤ ★★★ Washington Square Arch. Designed by Stanford White, the first arch here was built of wood in 1889 to commemorate the centennial of George Washington's inauguration; the current 1891 version is white marble. The statues of George Washington were done by Alexander Stirling Calder, father of modern artist and mobile-maker Alexander Calder. *Fifth Ave. and Waverly Place.*

⑥ ★★ The Row. Built in the 1830's for society's blue bloods, this is the longest string of Greek Revival townhouses in the country. Henry James's heroine in *Washington Square* lived here, as did many memorable characters in Edith Wharton's novels. By the early 20th century, the strip had become rundown and many of the Village's best-known "bohemians" moved in, including painters Edward Hopper and Thomas Eakins and writer John Dos Passos (all lived at #3). *1–26 Washington Sq. N. (btw. Fifth Ave. and University Place).*

⑦ ★ Caffe Reggio. The quintessential Village cafe—art-filled and cozy—claims to have brought the first espresso machine to the US. *119 MacDougal St. (at West 3rd. St.) www.caffereggio.com.* ☎ *212/475-9577. $.*

⑧ ★130 Macdougal St. This perfect little brick federal town house is where Louisa May Alcott probably wrote *Little Women.*

Minetta Street.

🍸 **Minetta Tavern.** Formerly a speakeasy called the Black Rabbit, this was a major literary hangout, serving up poetry-inspiring booze and spaghetti to such notables as Ezra Pound, e.e.cummings, and Ernest Hemingway in the '20s, and Allen Ginsberg and Jack Kerouac in the 50's. *At 113 MacDougal St.*

⓾ ★★★ **Minetta Street.** Listen carefully: A stream runs below this street and sometimes it's possible to hear it gurgling. When the stream was at street level, this was a muddy ghetto called "Little Africa" and inhabited entirely by free blacks from the 1820's to the 1910's. In 1863 when Civil War draft riots sparked the worst violence in the city's history, the residents of this street were able to successfully barricade it for five days against the hooligans who killed 105 African Americans in other neighborhoods.

⓫ ★ **Cherry Lane Theatre.** Poet Edna St. Vincent Millay and her artist peers converted an 1817 box factory into the Cherry Lane Playhouse in 1924. It's still a working theater. *38 Commerce St. (at Bedford St.). www.cherrylanetheatre. org.* ☎ *212/989-2020.*

⓬ **48 Commerce St.** Note the working gas lamp in front of this 1844 home. The New York Gas Light Company began laying gas pipes in 1823, and gas lamps—many with ornamental posts—continued to shine into the 20th century. *48 Commerce St. (at Barrow St.).*

⓭ ★ **St. Luke in the Fields.** This charming little church is a reconstruction of the original, which was built in 1822 and badly damaged by fire in 1981. One of the church's founding wardens was

Clement C. Moore, the author of *'Twas the Night Before Christmas. 487 Hudson St. (at Grove St.).*

⓮ ★ **Grove Court.** This charming gated mews was once considered a slum; it was built for working men around 1853, when it was known as "Mixed Ale Alley" (because residents could only afford to drink from the dregs at the "bottom of the barrel"). Today this is one of the city's most coveted addresses. *10–12 Grove St. (btw. Hudson and Bedford sts.).*

⓯ ★★ **17 Grove St.** This 1822 house is one of the last remaining wood-framed houses in the Village. The building across the street was used in the TV show *Friends* (Monica and the gang "lived" here). *17 Grove St. (at Bedford St.).*

⓰ ★ **West Bleecker Street Shopping District.** Bleecker Street, from Christopher to Bank Street, is a trendy boutique alley that's a heckuva lot of fun to stroll. *W. Bleecker St. (btw. Christopher and Bank sts.).*

The private entrance at Grove Court

Prospect Park & Park Slope

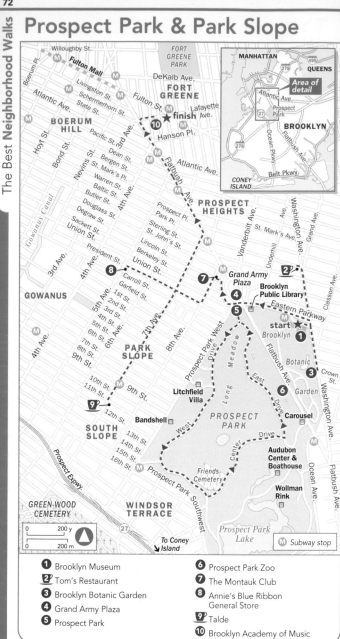

1. Brooklyn Museum
2. Tom's Restaurant
3. Brooklyn Botanic Garden
4. Grand Army Plaza
5. Prospect Park
6. Prospect Park Zoo
7. The Montauk Club
8. Annie's Blue Ribbon General Store
9. Talde
10. Brooklyn Academy of Music

The attractions in and around Prospect Park are well worth the 25-minute subway ride from midtown Manhattan. Expect gorgeous parkland designed by Frederick Law Olmsted and Calvert Vaux (the masterminds of Central Park), the city's second-largest art museum, plus lovely 19th-century brownstones and hip boutiques. START: Subway 2/3 to Eastern Parkway.

❶ ★★★ kids Brooklyn Museum.

In any other city, this spectacular museum would be *the* star attraction, but in New York it's often overlooked because of all the competition. The collection is New York's second-largest. Highlights include the stellar **ancient Egyptian collection**, the **Asian art collection** (which specializes in both classic and contemporary works from Japan), and the **Luce Center for American Art** (an "open storage" annex holding 9,000 works, from Tiffany lamps to 19th-century furniture by local artisans). Designed by architects McKim, Mead & White in 1897, the museum received a dramatic plaza complete with fountains in 2004. ◐ 2–3 hr. 200 Eastern Pkwy. (at Washington Ave.). www.brooklynmuseum.org. ☎ 718/638-5000. Admission $16 adults, $10 seniors and students, free for ages 19 and under. Thurs 11am–10pm, Fri–Sun and Wed 11am–6pm, first Sat of every month until 11pm. Subway: 2/3 to Eastern Pkwy.

❷ Tom's Restaurant.

Really a diner, flag-bedecked Tom's serves the best lemon poppy pancakes on the planet, and (a rarity these days) authentic New Yawk egg creams. Service is grandmotherly in its sweetness. Breakfast and lunch only. 782 Washington Ave. (at Sterling Place). ☎ 718/636-9728. $.

❸ ★★★ Brooklyn Botanic Garden.

This tranquil, elegant retreat is one of the most beautiful gardens in the city. It encompasses the **Cranford Rose Garden,** a Children's Garden, the **Osborne Garden** (3 acres/1.2 hectares of formal gardens), the **Fragrance Garden** (designed for the visually impaired but appreciated by all), and the **Japanese Hill-and-Pond Garden.** In colder weather, you can investigate one of the world's largest collections of bonsai in the **C. V. Starr Bonsai Museum** and indoor plants (everything from cacti to orchids) in the **Steinhardt Conservatory.** If you come in April or May, seek out the lush carpet of bluebells and check the website for the timing of the **Cherry Blossom Festival.** ◐ 1–2 hr. 1000 Washington Ave. (at Eastern Pkwy.). www.bbg.org. ☎ 718/623-7200. Admission $12 adults, $6 seniors and students, free for children 12 and under. Mar–Oct Tues–Fri 8am–6pm, Sat–Sun 10am–6pm; Nov–Feb until 4:30pm.

The Brooklyn Museum.

Soldiers' and Sailors' Memorial Arch at Prospect Park.

4 Grand Army Plaza. This multilane traffic circle and the tremendous **Soldiers' and Sailors' Memorial Arch** at its center may remind you of Paris's Place Charles de Gaulle and the Arc de Triomphe. The arch was built in 1892 to honor Union soldiers who died in the Civil War. *At the intersection of*

Flatbush Ave., Prospect Park W., Eastern Pkwy. and Vanderbilt Ave.

5 ★★★ kids Prospect Park. Central Park designers Frederick Law Olmstead and Calvert Vaux considered Prospect Park to be their masterpiece. The park has 562 acres (225 hectares) of woodland—including Brooklyn's last remaining virgin forest—plus meadows, bluffs, and ponds. For the best views, enter at Grand Army Plaza and walk to your right either on the park's ring road (called West Dr. here) or on the parallel pedestrian path to Meadowport Arch, and proceed to **Long Meadow.** Overlooking Long Meadow is **Litchfield Villa,** an 1857 mansion that became the headquarters for the New York parks system. Eventually West Drive turns into Center Drive, which will take you past the **Friends' Cemetery** Quaker burial ground. Center Drive leads to East Drive, which on its way back to Grand Army Plaza passes the 1906 Beaux Arts **boathouse;** the 1912 **carousel;** the **zoo** (see below); and **Lefferts Homestead Children's Historic House Museum** (☎ 718/789-2822), a 1783

Prospect Park's Boathouse.

Dutch farmhouse with a museum of period furniture and exhibits. *Bounded by Prospect Park W., Parkside Ave. and Flatbush Ave. www.prospectpark.org.* ☎ *718/965-8951.*

⑥ ★ kids Prospect Park Zoo. Families won't want to miss the zoo at the eastern end of the park. Children in particular take delight in encountering the animals up close, including wallabies and prairie dogs. ⏱ *1 hr. 450 Flatbush Ave. www.prospectparkzoo.com.* ☎ *718/399-7339. Admission $8 adults, $6 seniors, $5 children 3–12. Mon–Fri 10am–5pm, Sat–Sun 10am–5:30pm.*

⑦ ★ The Montauk Club. The northwestern side of Prospect Park is home to the upscale neighborhood of Park Slope, and its tree-lined streets are delightful to explore. Many of the late-19th-century brownstones have been lovingly restored (walk along Montgomery Place between Eighth Ave. and Prospect Park W. to see what we mean). If there were an award for most stunning building, it would go to the **Montauk Club,** which was designed in 1891 by architect Francis H. Kimball to resemble a Venetian palace. It's a private club. *25 Eighth Ave. (at Lincoln Place).* ☎ *718/638-0800.*

⑧ ★★ Annie's Blue Ribbon General Store. Fashion Institute of Technology prof Ann Cantrull sells handsome and giftable housewares, stationery, toys, and tchotchkes, most of them made in Brooklyn (and many NYC-themed). Souvenir hunters: you're welcome. *232 Fifth Ave (btw. Carroll and President sts.). www.blueribbongeneral store.com.*

Picnic in Prospect Park.

⑩ Talde. Chef/owner Dale Talde almost won Top Chef Masters—twice. But his food here proves he's a champ, mouthwatering Asian fusion fare, like pretzel-crunchy dumplings, and a peach-laden smoked shrimp curry. *369 Seventh Ave. www.taldebrooklyn.com.* ☎ *347/916-0031. $$–$$$.*

⑨ ★★★ Brooklyn Academy of Music. Head to nearby Fort Greene, home to this always entertaining and intellectually challenging pair of theaters. On the roster might be Peter Brooks' latest directing venture, dance by Anne Teresa De Keersmaeker, an opera, or a conversation with a trendsetter like Tina Fey or Anthony Bourdain. *Peter Jay Sharp Building, 30 Lafayette Ave. (btw. Ashland Place and St. Felix St.). www.bam.org.* ☎ *718/636-4100. Subway: 2/3/4/5/B/D/N/R/Q to Atlantic Ave.*

Williamsburg, Brooklyn

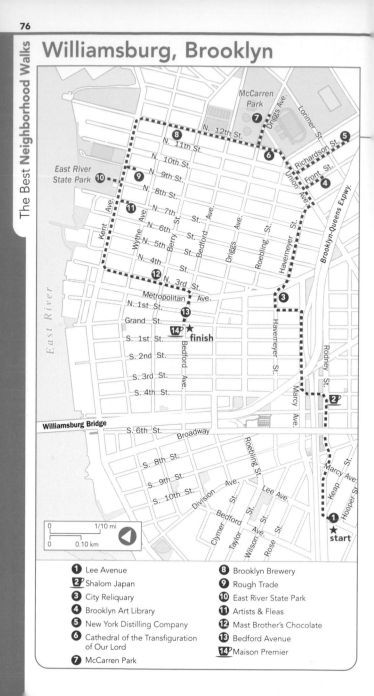

1. Lee Avenue
2. Shalom Japan
3. City Reliquary
4. Brooklyn Art Library
5. New York Distilling Company
6. Cathedral of the Transfiguration of Our Lord
7. McCarren Park
8. Brooklyn Brewery
9. Rough Trade
10. East River State Park
11. Artists & Fleas
12. Mast Brother's Chocolate
13. Bedford Avenue
14. Maison Premier

Hipsters and Hasidim—those are the primary residents of this beguiling neighborhood. While you won't find the elegant architecture that graces other areas of the city—Williamsburg was once mostly factories, warehouses, and hastily built low-rise apartment buildings for workers—you will encounter a neighborhood bursting with artistic energy, *joie de vivre . . .* and stark contrasts.
START: **Subway J, Z or M to Marcy Ave.**

❶ ★ Lee Avenue. This stretch, between Taylor and Heywood, is the commercial center of the largest Hasidic community (70,000-plus ultra-Orthodox Satmar Jews) anywhere. Hebrew lettering adorns storefronts; inside, goods include silver candlesticks and menorahs, wigs (married women must wear them), wide-brimmed black hats, and Eastern European noshes. You'll see many kids; families in this neighborhood average 5 to 7 children. ⏱ 40 min.

❷ ★★ Shalom Japan. An "authentically inauthentic" fusion resto that puts matzoh balls into ramen soup, and slathers sashimi with tahini—all to delicious effect. *310 S. 4th St. (at Rodney St.) www.shalomjapannyc.com.* ☎ *718/388-4012. $$.*

❸ ★★ City Reliquary. An itsy-bitsy museum, the Reliquary displays the ephemera of Big Apple life—a wooden brick from the last wood sidewalk in the city, branded seltzer bottles from long-gone delis, Statue of Liberty statuettes in every form imaginable, and more. A cabinet of nostalgia. ⏱ 30 min. *370 Metropolitan Ave. (at Havermeyer St.). www.cityreliquary.org.* ☎ *718/782-4842. Admission $5 adults, $4 seniors and students, free to children 12 and under. Thurs-Fri and Sun noon–6pm, Sat noon–8pm.*

❹ ★ Brooklyn Art Library. Home to the "Sketchbook Project,"

Nostalgic items at City Reliquary.

which collects hand-written (and -drawn) books from artists—including self-taught artists—from around the world (over 160,000 of books!). Step in to read one or two of these fascinating, one-of-a-kind tomes. ⏱ 30 min. *28 Frost St. (btw. Union and Lorimer Sts.) www.sketchbookproject.org.* ☎ *718/388-7941. Free. Tues–Sun 8888–4pm.*

❺ ★ New York Distilling Company. The first legal distilling company in the city since Prohibition leads free tours of its facilities on weekend afternoons. Afterwards, belly up to the bar (called **The Shanty**) for an expertly mixed cocktail, featuring the gins and ryes you just witnessed bubbling away. ⏱ 45 min. *79 Richardson St. (btw. Leonard and Lorimer sts.). www.*

The Brooklyn Brewery.

nydistilling.com. ☎ 718/878-3579. Free. Weekends 2:30–5:30pm.

❻ ★★★ Cathedral of the Transfiguration of our Lord. It was only after the end of World War II that sermons began to be delivered in English at this exquisite onion-domed Russian Orthodox church. It's still a gathering place for a community that originally emigrated in the 1920s from Europe's Carpathian Mountains (services are in Old Church Slavic, which is similar to Russian). If it's open, step inside to see a host of dazzling gold-painted religious icons; this is the only example of Byzantine Revival architecture on the East Coast. The church was featured in an episode of Seinfeld. ⏱ 20 min. At the corner of Union and 12th sts. Free admission. Hours vary.

❼ McCarren Park. This handsome park was a grungy outdoor bazaar for drug dealers in the 1960's and 1970's. While the entire city was in decline then, Williamsburg was particularly hard-hit, with several of its factories closing. Many police officers colluded with the dealers in the dangerous park (nicknamed "The Killing Fields" back then), until a brave cop named

Frank Serpico—you might have seen the film about him or read the book—exposed the corruption in the neighborhood.

❽ ★ Brooklyn Brewery. Another booze tour! As at the distillery, you'll be both well informed and tipsy by the end. The brewery was founded in 1988 by Steve Hindy, who learned to home brew out of necessity while serving as a correspondent for the Associated Press in the dry Middle East. ⏱ 30 min. 79 North 11th St. (btw. Berry St. and Wythe Ave.). www.brooklyn brewery.com. Free tours weekends between noon and 6pm, weekday tastings and tours at 5pm for $25.

❾ ★ Rough Trade. London's punk rock mecca spawned a transatlantic outlet, and like the original it's filled with records (yes, vinyl ones!) and has an intimate theater in the back for topnotch concerts in a number of genres. Look up: Freight shipping containers line the walls and are used for some of the second-floor offices. ⏱ 20 min. 64 North 9th St. (btw. Kent and Wythe Aves.). www.roughtrade.com.

❿ ★★ East River State Park. Wander into this small park for spectacular views of the Manhattan skyline. If it's a Saturday between May and November, the fab food festival **Smorgasburg** will be in session. Entrance on Kent Ave.

⓫ ★★ Artists & Fleas. In this hangar-like space, filled with small tables piled high with wares, you'll find all sorts of chic and/or quirky clothing, accessories, and household goods, often sold by the artist who made them. ⏱ 30 min. 70 North 7th St. (btw. Kent and Wythe Aves.). www.artistsandfleas.com. Sat–Sun 10am–7pm.

⓬ ★★★ Mast Brother's Chocolate. As you walk in, the mere

A street mural near Bedford Avenue.

smell will send your salivary glands into overdrive. We recommend not only buying here, but taking the absorbing tour, which covers the history of the founding brothers (who used blow dryers to cure cocoa beans in their first apartment-made bars) as well as the inner workings of this small factory, which puts out 2000 bars a day. It all ends with an elaborate tasting, during which visitors sample raw product—crafted from beans from different parts of the globe—and then finished bars, with such

additions as tarragon or coffee. ⏱ *45 min. 11 North 3rd St. (near Berry St.). www.mastbrothers.com. Hourly tours $10. Daily 11am–5pm.*

⓭ ★★ **Bedford Avenue.** Billyburg's main drag is a gallery and boutique-lined fun fest, with shops from multi-national chains (like Apple and Madewell), along with cute local concerns. Don't skip the **Mini-Mall** (at 218 Bedford), which holds a terrific bookstore, a well-curated vintage clothing shop, and accessories shops with real flair. In the streets off Bedford, look for street murals—a number of name artists paint them to help up the prices on the pieces they're selling in galleries (no guerilla art here!).

⓮ ★★ **Maison Premier.** In 2016, the James Beard Association named this the best "bar program" in the U.S.A. Translation: the cocktails are scintillating. But we're also big fans of the seafood-heavy menu and décor, both of which bring the best of New Orleans to Brooklyn. *298 Bedford Ave. (btw. Grand and 1st St.). www.maisonpremier.com.* ☎ *347-335-0446. $$–$$$.*

Quirky merchandise at Artists & Fleas.

Chinatown & The Lower East Side

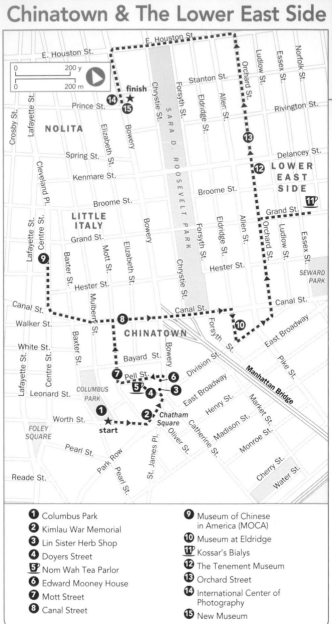

1 Columbus Park

2 Kimlau War Memorial

3 Lin Sister Herb Shop

4 Doyers Street

5 Nom Wah Tea Parlor

6 Edward Mooney House

7 Mott Street

8 Canal Street

9 Museum of Chinese in America (MOCA)

10 Museum at Eldridge

11 Kossar's Bialys

12 The Tenement Museum

13 Orchard Street

14 International Center of Photography

15 New Museum

Long known for its vibrant street life, the Lower East Side was also home to notorious slums (including the Five Points) where Irish, Italian, Jewish, and Chinese immigrants crowded into tenements. Although much survives from that era—including many of the tenement buildings—today the neighborhood buzzes with the energy of new restaurants, galleries, bars, and live-music clubs. START: **Subway 4/5/6 to Brooklyn Bride or J/Z to Chambers St.**

Ducks hanging in a Chinatown restaurant's front window.

❶ ★ **Columbus Park.** This park lies where New York's worst slum, known as Mulberry Bend, once stood, surrounded by tenements with such names as Bone Alley, Kerosene Row, and Bandits' Roost. Most of the houses were torn down in the early 20th century. Today the park is filled with Chinese immigrants practicing tai chi and playing games of chance at the stone tables. It's quite a scene. *Bounded by Mosco, Mulberry, Bayard and Baxter sts.*

❷ **Kimlau War Memorial.** This memorial arch in Chatham Square was erected in 1962 to honor the Chinese Americans who gave their lives fighting in World War II. The square also contains an imposing statue of Lin Zexu, a 19th-century antidrug hero in China. *Chatham Sq.*

❸ ★★ **Lin Sister Herb Shop.** This three-story apothecary is a marvel. A wall of wooden drawers, each containing medicinal herbs, dominates the first floor. On the upper levels, reflexology massage and acupuncture treatments are offered, and a homeopathic doctor is available for consultations. *4 Bow-*

Acupuncture model at a Chinese pharmacy.

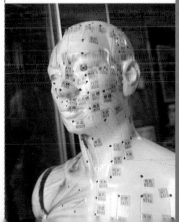

ery (at Division St.). www.lin sister.com. ☎ 212/962-5417.

④ ★★ Doyers Street. As you walk along Bowery, keep an eye out for Doyers Street, a narrow, crooked alleyway once notorious for activity by gangs known as tongs. The bend in the street allowed the thugs to jump victims and attack them with hatchets (hence the term "hatchet man"). During the week enter door #9 and head downstairs to see a warren of bustling employment agencies, where new Chinese immigrants go to find jobs.

⑤ ★★ Nom Wah Tea Parlor. Nom Wah opened in 1920, making it the oldest dim sum joint in Chinatown. Formica tables, wood booths, red chairs—this oldie is definitely a goodie. Order the egg roll, which it claims is the "original." Whether it is or not, you'll probably not find one as fresh and light elsewhere. 13 Doyers St. (btw. Bowery and Pell St.). www.nomwah.com. ☎ 212/962-6047. $.

⑥ Edward Mooney House. This Georgian brick structure, painted red, is the oldest row house in the city, dating from George Washington's New York days. Wealthy merchant Edward Mooney had the house built in 1785 on property abandoned by a Tory during the American Revolution. 18 Bowery (at Pell St.).

⑦ ★ Mott Street. The heart of old Chinatown, this is the epicenter of the boisterous yearly Chinese New Year celebrations—and a nifty place to wander and shop any time of year. Some addresses to note: no. 17, where, down a set of steps, you will dine in grungy glory on such Chinese-American classics as sweet and sour chicken at legendary **Wop Hop; New Age Designer** at no. 38, for a traditional Chinese cheongsam (dress) made of colorful Chinese silk for around $400; and **Aji Ichiban** at no. 37, a Hong Kong chain that sells unusual candies and dried fish and fruits—all of which can be sampled on site, free. A charming outpost of the famous Taiwanese chain **Ten Ren Tea** (at #75) has a museum-worthy display of teapots, and do stop by the dazzling **Chopstick Shop** (at #50). Respectful visitors are welcome at the **Eastern Buddhist Temple** (#64).

⑧ Canal Street. From West Broadway to the Manhattan Bridge, this is one of the city's liveliest and most congested thoroughfares. Stalls hawk everything from

Chopstick shop in Chinatown.

Chinatown & The Lower East Side

Vendor on Canal Street.

"designer" handbags to electronics. **Kam Man,** at no. 200, is our favorite stop: a combo grocery/electronics/homegoods superstore, selling wares from across Asia.

9 ★★ kids Museum of Chinese in America (MOCA). It is difficult to comprehend the cruel hardships that the first generations of Chinese suffered in New York. This museum documents the history and culture of the Chinese in America from the early 1800s to the present. ⏱ *45 min. 215 Centre St. (btw. Howard and Grand sts.). www.mocanyc.org.* ☎ *212/619-4785. Admission $10 adults, $5 seniors and students, free for kids 12 and under. Tues–Sun 11am–6pm, Thurs until 9pm. Subway: N/R/Q/J/Z/6 to Canal St.*

10 ★★ Museum at Eldridge. When this former synagogue was built by Eastern European Jews in 1887, it was the most magnificent on the Lower East Side. Its congregation once included such luminaries as Eddie Cantor, Jonas Salk, and Edward G. Robinson. Over the years, however, membership declined, and the structure fell into disrepair in the 1950s. A recent $20-million renovation restored the building to its former glory—and then some. One highlight amendment to the original Herter Brothers design is a new central window by celebrated artist Kiki Smith.

⏱ *20 min. 12 Eldridge St. (btw. Canal and Division sts.). www.eldridgestreet. org.* ☎ *212/219-0302. Admission $14 adults, $10 seniors and students, $8 children 5–18, free for children 4 and under; free for all Mon. Sun–Thurs 10am–5pm, Fri 10am–3pm. Subway: B/D to Grand St. or 6.*

11 Kossar's Bialys. A true New York treat, bialys are like bagels but hole-less and less uniform in shape. Kossar's is the oldest bialy bakery in the USA and they're still using their original recipes—why fix what isn't broken? *367 Grand St. (btw. Essex and Norfolk sts).* ☎ *212/473-4810. $.*

Guided tour at the Tenement Museum.

⑫ ★★★ The Tenement Museum. This tremendously moving museum documents the lives of immigrant residents in a six-story tenement built in 1863 at 97 Orchard Street (accessible only via fascinating guided tours). The tenement rooms are eerily authentic, and for good reason: 97 Orchard was essentially boarded up from 1935 to 1987; when it was finally reopened, everything was exactly as it had been left, a virtual time capsule of 1935 tenement life. Artifacts found range from the mundane (medicine tins and Russian cigarettes) to the personal (a 1922 Ouija board and an infant's button-up shoe). Visitors choose among several tours, each of which profiles a different family and/or apartment (there are also neighborhood walking tours). Book your visit online at least a week in advance—this is one of New York's most popular museums. ① 1–1½ hr. 103 Orchard St. (at Delancey St.). www.tenement. org. ☎ 212/982-8420. Tours $25 adults, $20 seniors and students. Tours daily.

⑬ ★★ Orchard Street. In the 19th century, this street was a vast outdoor marketplace lined with rows of pushcarts. Today, stores for imported (and discounted) luggage, lingerie, suits, and dresses have replaced the carts, but in the spirit of tradition, some shop owners are still willing to haggle over prices. Also lining the street: stylish little boutiques, art galleries, and cafes. It's a brand-new melting pot. On Sundays, Orchard is closed to vehicular traffic between Delancey and Houston streets so that wares can be sold in the open air. Stop in at the **Lower East Side Visitor Center** at 54 Orchard St. (☎ 212/ 226-9010; www.lowereastside.org) for a map of the 124 art galleries in the neighborhood (with info on current shows).

⑭ ★ International Center of Photography. The art of photography is examined through a sociological lens at this smartly curated museum. That might mean an exhibit on what it means to be a photographer in an image-saturated world; or one on the intersection of journalism and photography. ICP is also an important educational institution and owns some 50,000–plus prints. ① 1 hr. 250 Bowery (near Prince St.). www. icp.org. ☎ 212/857-0000. Admission $14 adults, $12 seniors, $10 students, free for children 14 and under. Tues–Thurs and Sat–Sun 10am–6pm, Fri 10am–9pm. Subway: 6 to Spring St.; N/R to Prince St.

⑮ ★ New Museum. The seven stories of the New Museum of contemporary art, designed by Tokyo–based architects Kazuyo Sejima and Ryue Nishizawa (aka SANAA), rise above the tenement buildings of the Lower East Side like boxes haphazardly piled upon one another. The offbeat exterior reflects the character of the exhibitions inside by new and emerging artists. ① 1 hr. 235 Bowery (at Prince St.). www.newmuseum.org. ☎ 212/219-1222. Admission $14 adults, $12 seniors, $10 students, free for children 18 and under; free for all Thurs 7–9pm. Wed and Fri–Sun 11am–6pm; Thurs 11am–9pm. Subway: 6 to Spring St.; N/R to Prince St. ●

5 The Best **Shopping**

Shopping **Best Bets**

Best **Food Store**
Kalustyan's, *123 Lexington Ave.* *(p 94)*

Best **Place to Deck Out Your Dream House**
ABC Carpet & Home, *881 and 888 Broadway (p 96)*

Best **Footwear**
Jeffrey New York, *449 W. 14th St.* *(p 92)*

Best **All-Around Department Store**
Bloomingdale's, *1000 Third Ave.* *(p 92)*

Best **Browsing**
MoMA Store, *44 W. 53rd St. (p 96)*

Best **Toy Store**
Toy Tokyo, *91 Second Ave. (p 98)*

Best **Men's Designer Clothes**
Bergdorf Goodman for Men, *754 Fifth Ave. (p 91)*

Best **Women's Designer Clothes**
Bergdorf Goodman, *754 Fifth Ave.* *(p 91)*

Best **Clothing Boutiques**
Kisan Concept Store, *125 Greene St. (p 93)*; and Opening Ceremony, *35 Howard St. (p 93)*

Best **Cheap & Trendy Clothes**
Topshop, *478 Broadway (p 93)*; and UNIQLO, *666 Fifth Ave. (p 93)*

Best **Vintage Jewelry**
Pippin, *72 Orchard St. (p 97)*

Best **Wine & Liquor**
Astor Wines, *399 Lafayette St.* *(p 94)*

Best **Deals on Electronics**
B&H Photo-Video-Pro Audio, *420 Ninth Ave. (p 92)*

Best **Beauty Products**
C. O. Bigelow, *414 Sixth Ave.* *(p 90)*

Sales-Tax Lowdown

The sales tax in New York City is 8.875% (4.5% for city sales tax, 4% for New York State tax, plus an additional surcharge). **No sales tax at all is charged for clothing and footwear purchases under $110.** If you have an item shipped, be sure to get proper documentation of the sale and keep the receipts handy until the merchandise arrives at your door.

Previous page: Chic footwear at the Camper store in SoHo.

Downtown Shopping

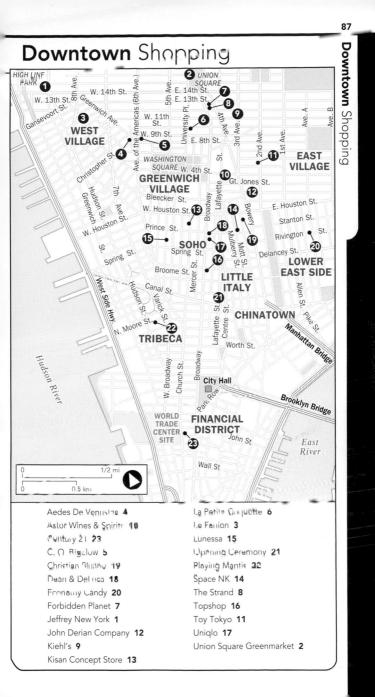

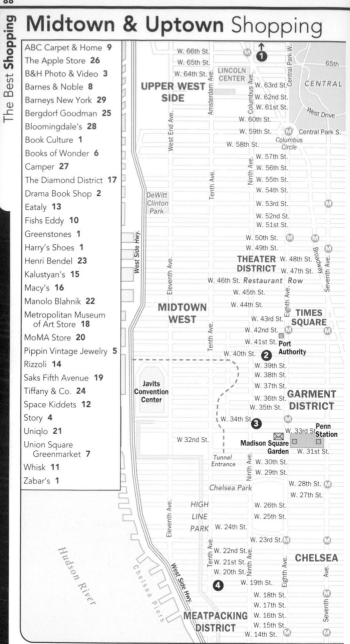

The Best Shopping

Midtown & Uptown Shopping

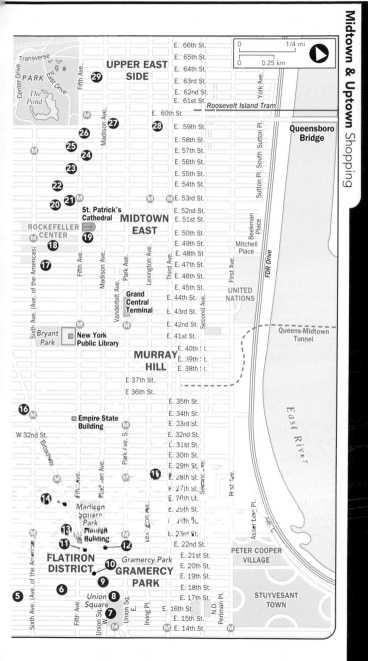

Shopping A to Z

C. O. Bigelow, the nation's oldest apothecary shop.

Beauty/Apothecary

★★ **C. O. Bigelow** GREENWICH VILLAGE Its motto—"If you can't get it anywhere else, try Bigelow's"—is right on the money. This 162-year-old apothecary, oldest in the nation, carries unusual brands, plus its own great line of personal-care products. *414 Sixth Ave. (btw. 8th and 9th sts.). www.bigelowchemists.com. ☎ 212/533-2700. AE, DISC, MC, V. Subway: A/C/E/F/M to W. 4th St.*

★ **Kiehl's** EAST VILLAGE This 150-plus-year-old firm's skin- and hair-care products have a cult following, and the store's free product samples add to its quirky charm. Formerly family-run, Kiehl's is now owned by L'Oréal. *109 Third Ave. (btw. 13th and 14th sts.). www.kiehls. com. ☎ 212/677-3171. AE, DC, MC, V. Subway: 4/5/6 to Union Sq.*

★ **Space NK** SOHO This British-based shop has culled the best of the best product lines and put them all in a soothing environment. It has an added location on the Upper East Side as well as spaces in Bloomingdale's (p 92). *99 Greene St. (btw. Prince and Spring sts.). www.spacenk.com. ☎ 212/ 941-4200. AE, DISC, MC, V. Subway: N/R to Prince St. or 6 to Spring St.*

Books

★★ **Barnes & Noble Union Square** UNION SQUARE This red-brick, terra-cotta relic from 1881 holds one of the chain's most impressive Manhattan stores. *Century* magazine was published here in the late 19th century. Other branches at Fifth Ave. and 45th St. and Broadway and 88th St. *33 E. 17th St. (btw. Broadway and Park Ave.). www.bn.com.*

Antique Districts

If you're into antiquing, the best strategy is to head for areas where such stores tend to cluster. One of the best areas is Greenwich Village, particularly **10th Street between Broadway and University Place** (take the 4/5/6, N/Q/R, or L subways to Union Sq.); stores on the block specialize in Scandinavian antiques, French Art Deco, Mid-Century Modern, Neoclassical furnishings and those from the Biedermeier school. There's also a flock of antique stores near the massive **Manhattan Art and Antiques Center** (1050 Second Ave. btw. 55th and 56th; subways 4/5/6 or N/Q/R to 59th St.). Best pickings are near Second Avenue on 59th, 60th, and 61st streets.

☎ 212/255-0810. AE, DC, DISC,
MC, V. Subway: 4/5/6 to Union Sq.

★★ **Book Culture** UPPER WEST
SIDE   A friendly, independent
store with a wide range of books
and a wonderfully knowledgeable
staff. *450 Columbus Ave. (btw. 81st
and 82nd St.). www.bookculture.com.*
☎ *212/595-1962. AE, DC, DISC,
MC, V. Subway: B/D to 79th St.*

★ **Drama Book Shop** THEATER
DISTRICT   The play's the thing,
and this little performing-arts bookstore sells thousands of plays, from
Greek tragedies to this year's hits.
*250 W. 40th St. (btw. Eighth and
Ninth aves.). www.dramabookshop.
com.* ☎ *212/944-0595. AE, MC, V.
Subway: A/C/E to 42nd St.*

★★ **Rizzoli** FLATIRON DISTRICT
This gorgeous bookstore is an
atmospheric place to browse for
high-end visual art and design
books, plus quality fiction and
gourmet cookbooks. *1133 Broadway (at 26th St.). www.rizzolibook
store.com.* ☎ *212/759-2424. AE,
MC, V. Subway: N/R to 28th St.*

★★★ **The Strand** UNION
SQUARE   This local legend is worth
a visit for its staggering "18 miles of
books," new and used titles at up
to 85% off list price. *828 Broadway
(at 12th St.). www.strandbooks.com.*

Refined book-browsing at Rizzoli.

☎ *212/473-1452. AE, DC, DISC,
MC, V. Subway: L/N/R/4/5/6 to
Union Sq.*

Department Stores
★ **Barneys New York** MIDTOWN
EAST   One week it's on the runway, the next it's being sold at Barney's. Fashion at its most cutting
edge . . . and pricey. *660 Madison
Ave. (at 61st St.). www.barneys.com.*
☎ *212/826-8900. AE, MC, V.
Subway: N/R to Fifth Ave.*

★★ **Bergdorf Goodman**
MIDTOWN   The place for ladies

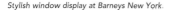

Stylish window display at Barneys New York.

who lunch and anyone who reveres fashion and clothes built to last. The **men's store** across the street (745 Fifth Ave.) has a great selection. *754 Fifth Ave. (at 58th St.). www.bergdorfgoodman.com.* ☎ *800/558-1855. AE, DC, MC, V. Subway: E/F to Fifth Ave.*

★★ **Bloomingdale's** MIDTOWN EAST Packed to the gills with goods, Bloomie's is more accessible and affordable than Barneys, Bergdorf, or Saks. There's a SoHo outpost too, at 504 Broadway. *1000 Third Ave. (Lexington Ave. at 59th St.). www. bloomingdales.com.* ☎ *212/705-2000. AE, MC, V. Subway: 4/5/6 to 59th St.*

★ **Henri Bendel** MIDTOWN Set inside a gorgeous landmark building, Bendel's sells funky and frilly accessories and homegoods, but no clothing. *712 Fifth Ave. (btw. 55th and 56th sts.). www.henribendel.com.* ☎ *212/247-1100. AE, DC, DISC, MC, V. Subway: N/R to Fifth Ave.*

Macy's HERALD SQUARE The size is unmanageable and the service is clueless, but they do sell *everything.* And *everything* goes on sale, at some point or another. *151 W. 34th St. (at Broadway). www.macys.com.* ☎ *212/695-4400. AE, MC, V. Subway: B/D/F/N/Q/R/1/2/3/ to 34th St.*

★ **Saks Fifth Avenue** MIDTOWN This legendary flagship store stocks big-name designers in fashion and accessories, with price tags to match. Look for smart house brands on the fourth and fifth floors. The make-up selection is the most wide-ranging in the city, with many European brands. *611 Fifth Ave. (btw. 49th and 50th sts.). www.saksfifthavenue.com.* ☎ *212/753-4000. AE, DC, DISC, MC, V. Subway: B/D/F/Q to 47th–50th sts./ Rockefeller Center; E/F to Fifth Ave.*

Electronics
★ **The Apple Store** MIDTOWN You know the drill: lots of tech, all laid out on tables for you to play with. But what's special about this store is its stunning architecture: Its glass cube top is the most photographed shop in the city. *767 Fifth Ave. (at 59th St.). www.apple.com.* ☎ *212/336-1440. AE, DISC, MC, V. Subway N/R to Fifth Ave.*

★★★ **B&H Photo-Video-Pro Audio** GARMENT DISTRICT The best place on the East Coast for deep discounts on cameras, TV's, computers, and other electronics. With 50% of their sales now online, service has become much less rushed (the salespeople are real experts). *Note:* Closed Saturdays. *420 Ninth Ave. (at 34th St.). www. bhphotovideo.com.* ☎ *800/606-6969. AE, DISC, MC, V. Subway: A/C/E to 34th St.*

Fashion
★ **Century 21** FINANCIAL DISTRICT It's easy to get addicted to the seriously discounted designer clothes here—just don't expect to be pampered or bathed in flattering lighting. Also at Broadway and 67th St. *22 Cortlandt St. (btw. Broadway and Church St.). www.c21stores. com.* ☎ *212/227-9092. AE, MC, V. Subway: 1/2/3/4/5/M to Fulton St.; A/C to Broadway/Nassau St.; E to Chambers St.*

★★★ **Christian Siriano** NOLITA The *Project Runway* star learned his TV lessons well: Create clothing that flatters all types of women and price the goods to move. You'll find many items at this store, the only one he has, that you won't find in the department stores that now carry his brand. *252 Elizabeth St. (btw. Prince St. and Houston). www. christiansiriano.com.* ☎ *212/775-8494. Subway: 6 to Bleecker St.*

★★ **Jeffrey New York** MEAT-PACKING DISTRICT This outpost of the famed Atlanta megaboutique may be pricey as all get-out,

Discounts on everything at Century 21.

but the staff is warm and friendly. The fantastic shoe selection is catnip to style hounds. *449 W. 14th St. (at 10th Ave.). www.jeffreynewyork. com.* ☎ *212/206-1272. AE, MC, V. Subway: A/C/E/L to 14th St.*

★★ Kisan Concept Store

SOHO   Arriving from Paris by way of Iceland, this shop sells not only "high-street" European women's wear but art books, shoes, a few men's items, and a breathtaking selection of fine kids' clothes. *125 Greene St. (btw. Prince and Houston sts.). www.kisanstore.com.* ☎ *212/ 475-2470. AE, MC, V. Subway: R/W to Prince St.*

★★ Opening Ceremony

CHINATOWN/SOHO   For many the top clothing boutique in the city, Opening Ceremony has fun, of the moment designs from all over the world, plus a house line that's smart, good-looking, and eminently wearable. It also has a location in the Ace Hotel. *35 Howard St. (near Broadway). www.openingceremony. us.* ☎ *212/219-2688. AE, MC, V. Subway: N/R/6 to Canal St.*

★ Topshop

SOHO   Your teenagers may drag you to this British megastore, but don't despair: Shopping at Topshop is delicious fun. Yes, a rock-star aesthetic predominates, from fringed suede to Edwardian puffy shirts, but you'll also find wearable separates like tailored boyfriend jackets and on-trend little black dresses. And the stuff is priced to move! *478 Broadway (near Spring St.). www.topshop. com.* ☎ *212/966-9555. AE, DISC, MC, V. Subway: 6 to Spring St.; N/R to Canal St.*

★ UNIQLO

MIDTOWN   The largest UNIQLO on the planet (there are also outposts in Soho, on 34th and 53rd sts.) this Fifth Avenue mothership is always packed. Known as Japan's answer to the Gap, UNIQLO specializes in smartly constructed basics, like the perfect black cotton V-neck shirt. *666 Fifth Ave. (at 53rd St.).* ☎ *917/237-8800. AE, DC, DISC, MC, V. Subway: N/R to Prince St.; 6 to Spring St.*

Midtown's UNIQLO is the chain's largest store.

Delectable cheeses at Eataly.

Food & Wine
★★ Astor Wines & Spirits

EAST VILLAGE   With a deep stock and great values, this spacious downtown institution not only features hard-to-find wines but has a vast collection of varied spirits at world-beating prices. *399 Lafayette St. (at E.4th St.). www.astorwines. com.* ☎ *212/674-7500. Subway: B/D/F/M to Broadway-Lafayette St.*

★ Dean & DeLuca SOHO   From
excellent cheese, meat, fish, and dessert counters to fresh sushi and luscious prepared foods—everything you'd need for a nosh. *560 Broadway (at Prince St.). www.dean-deluca. com.* ☎ *212/226-6800. AE, DISC, MC, V. Subway: N/R to Prince St.*

★★★ Economy Candy LOWER
EAST SIDE   All of the obscure candies you gorged on as a kid, plus superb halvah and dried fruits, all at, yes, economy prices. A trip back in time. *108 Rivington St. (btw. Delancey and Norfolk sts.). www.economy candy.com.* ☎ *212/254-1531. AE, MC, V. Subway: F to Delancey St.*

★★★ Eataly FLATIRON DISTRICT
Created by Mario Batali and Joe

and Lidia Bastianich, Eataly is an Italian market on steroids. Aisle upon groaning aisle is stocked with imported pastas, olive oils and vinegars, fresh mozzarella, pastries, coffee, books, and more. You can buy, or dine in at six different on-site Italian eateries. In 2016, an outlet opened downtown (see p 16). *200 Fifth Ave. (at 23rd St.). www.eataly. com.* ☎ *212/229-2560. AE, MC, V. Market daily 10am–11pm. Restaurants daily lunch and dinner. Subway: N/R/6 to 23rd St.*

★★★ Kalustyan's MIDTOWN
This 72-year-old international market just keeps growing. At the close of 2015, it added 6,500 square feet, but the aisles still feel cramped, crammed with goodies from all over the globe: Korean chili paste, candied violets, Sicilian pistachios, 100 different types of salt, and every type of spice known to man. *123 Lexington Ave. (btw. 28th and 29th sts.). www.kalustyans.com.* ☎ *212/685-3451. AE, MC, V. Subway: 6 to 28th St.*

★★★ Union Square Green-
market UNION SQUARE   At Manhattan's largest farmer's market, you'll find fresh produce from

Union Square Greenmarket.

Zabar's, the Upper West Side's renowned food specialty store.

upstate and New Jersey farms, fish just off the boat from Long Island, artisanal cheeses, home-cured meats, plants, and organic herbs and spices. I've seen star chefs here with wheelbarrows in tow. Open daytime year-round on Monday, Wednesday, Friday, and Saturday. *In Union Sq. www.grownyc.org.* ☎ *212/788-7476. No credit cards. Subway: 4/5/6/N/Q/R/W to Union Sq.*

★★ **Zabar's** UPPER WEST SIDE The one-and-only Zabar's is the place to go for great smoked salmon and all the works—not to mention terrific prepared foods, gourmet edibles, coffees, cheeses, you name it. *2245 Broadway (at 80th St.). www.zabars.com.* ☎ *212/496-1234. AE, DC, MC, V. Subway: 1 to 79th St.*

Gifts

★ **Forbidden Planet** UNION SQUARE Know someone who lives in a fantasy world? This superstore of comics and manga holds a gift for them, whether it be an action figure, a rare graphic novel, or a costume. *832 Broadway (btw. 12th and 13th*

sts.). www.fpnyc.com. ☎ *212/473-1576. AE, MC, V. Subway: L/N/R/4/5/6 to 14th St./Union Sq.*

★★ **John Derian Company** EAST VILLAGE Fabulous decoupage items, colorful candleholders handmade in Paris, and terra cotta pottery are but a few of the delicious treats here. *6 E. 2nd St. (btw. Second Ave. and the Bowery). www.johnderian.com.* ☎ *212/677-3917. AE, MC, V. Subway: 6 to Bleecker St., F/M to Second Ave.*

★★ **Le Fanion** GREENWICH VILLAGE Beautiful French Country pottery in a charming Village shop. *299 W. 4th St. (at Bank St.). www.lefanion.com.* ☎ *212/463-8760. AE, MC, V. Subway: 1/2/3 at 14th St.*

★★ **Metropolitan Museum of Art Store** MIDTOWN Great for jewelry, china, books, toys, textiles, umbrellas, and objets d'art modeled on the Met's collection. See website for branch locations. *15 W. 49th St. (at Rockefeller Center). www.metmuseum.org/store.* ☎ *212/332-1360. AE, DISC, MC, V. Subway: B/D/F/M to 47th–50th sts./Rockefeller Center.*

★★★ MoMA Store MIDTOWN
The Museum of Modern Art store stocks fabulous, unique gifts, from silk scarves with Frank Lloyd Wright designs to Eames chairs. The Christmas ornaments are gorgeous. See website for branch locations. *44 W. 53rd St. (btw. Fifth and Sixth aves.). www.momastore.org. ☎ 212/767-1050. AE, DISC, MC, V. Subway: E/M to Fifth Ave./53rd St.*

★★★ Story CHELSEA
Now here's a concept: Story changes its entire inventory every two months or so, basing what it sells around a theme (such as "Feminism" or "Emojis," recently). The "curators" find hip articles from unusual sources—I can't tell you exactly *what* you'll buy here, but I know you'll be tempted to buy. *144 Tenth Ave. (at 19th St.). www.thisisstory. com. ☎ 212/242-4853. AE, DISC, MC, V. Subway: A/C/E/L to Eighth Ave./14th St.*

Home Design & Housewares
★★★ ABC Carpet & Home
FLATIRON DISTRICT This magical (and costly) two-building emporium is the ultimate home fashions and furnishings store, with everything

ABC Carpet & Home.

from zillion-thread-count sheets to enchanting children's furniture. *881 and 888 Broadway (at 19th St.). www. abchome.com. ☎ 212/473-3000. AE, DISC, MC, V. Subway: L/N/R/ 4/5/6 to 14th St./Union Sq.*

★ Fishs Eddy FLATIRON
DISTRICT Come here for vintage and reproduction dishes, flatware, and glasses. *889 Broadway (at 19th St.). www.fishseddy.com.*

Fishs Eddy's New York–centric designs.

☎ 212/420-9020, AE, MC, V. Subway: L/N/R/4/5/6 to 14th St./Union Sq.

★★ **Whisk** FLATIRON DISTRICT The best kitchenware store in the city, it has every gadget, pot, and pan you'd ever need—and plenty you didn't *know* you needed until you walked in. Also in Brooklyn. *933 Broadway (btw. 21st and 22nd sts.). www.whisknyc.com.* ☎ *212/477-8680. AE, MC, V. Subway: N/R/6 to 23rd St.*

Jewelry & Precious Stones
The Diamond District MIDTOWN This is the heart of the city's diamond trade, although many merchants deal in semiprecious stones, too. If you know your four C's, it's a great place to get a deal on diamonds; if you don't, stick to window-shopping. Most shops open Monday to Friday only. *47th St. (btw. Fifth and Sixth aves.). Subway: B/D/F/M to Rockefeller Center.*

★★ **Lunessa** SOHO The fun of shopping here isn't just finding great jewelry (though they do have that). It's going to the "gem bar" and creating your own glam look on the spot. *100 Thompson St. (near Prince St.). www.lunessa.com.* ☎ *917/305-0510. AE, MC, V. Subway: N, R to Prince St.*

★ **Pippin Vintage Jewelry** CHELSEA From stately pearls to funky Bakelite, this gem of a shop carries it all. Also check out Pippin Home, a small shop selling antiques and home furnishings, behind the jewelry store. *112 W. 17th St. (btw. Sixth and Seventh aves.) www.pippinvintage.com.* ☎ *212/505-5159. AE, MC, V. Subway: A/E to 14th St.*

★★ **Tiffany & Co.** MIDTOWN Deservedly famous, this iconic multilevel store carries jewelry, watches, tableware, and stemware, and a variety of gift items. Love the silver yo-yo! *727 Fifth Ave. (at 57th St.). www.tiffany.com.* ☎ *212/755-8000. AE, DC, DISC, MC, V. Subway: N/R to Fifth Ave.*

Lingerie
★★ **La Petite Coquette** GREENWICH VILLAGE Expert bra fitters are in charge, and the goods range from great neutral underthings to gear that would make a dominatrix blush. *51 University Place (btw. 9th and 10th sts.). www.lapetitcoquette.com.* ☎ *212/473-2478. AE, DC, DISC. Subway: 4/5/6/L/N/Q/R to Union Sq.*

Perfumes/Scents
★★ **Aedes De Venustas** GREENWICH VILLAGE Evoking a romantic boudoir out of the Victorian era, this whimsical spot offers exotic and hard-to-find scents. *7 Greenwich Ave. (at Christopher St.). www.aedes.com.* ☎ *212/206-8674. AE, MC, V. Subway: 1 to Christopher St.*

Shoes
★★★ **Camper** MIDTOWN Chic chunky footwear, soothing to the sole, in a range of cool colors: these are the hallmarks of the men's and women's shoes made by this Spanish chain. Also in Soho. *635 Madison Ave (at 59th St.). www.camper.com.* ☎ *212/339-0078. AE, DISC, MC, V. Subway: 4/5/6/N/Q/R to 59th St.*

★ **Harry's Shoes** UPPER WEST SIDE This old-school store doesn't sell sex (à la Manolo, below); it sells shoes. Great selection of comfortable styles. **Harry's Shoes for Kids** is a half-block away at 2315 Broadway. *2299 Broadway (at 83rd St.). www.harrys-shoes.com.* ☎ *866/442-7797. AE, DISC, MC, V. Subway: 1 to 79th St. or 86th St.*

★★ **Manolo Blahnik** MIDTOWN These wildly sexy women's shoes could turn anyone into a foot fetishist. *31 W. 54th St. (btw. Fifth and Sixth aves.).* ☎ *212/582-3007. AE, MC, V. Subway: E/F to Fifth Ave.*

Toys, Children's Books & Clothing

★★ **kids Books of Wonder** UNION SQUARE Remember the charming bookstore in the Meg Ryan rom-com *You've Got Mail*? It was inspired by Books of Wonder, and the real thing is just as magical (and jam-packed with great kiddie reads). *18 W. 18th St. (btw. Fifth and Sixth aves.). www.booksofwonder. com.* ☎ *212/989-3270. AE, MC, V. Subway: L/N/R/4/5/6 to 14th St./ Union Sq.*

★ **Greenstones** UPPER WEST SIDE Greenstones has a wide variety of trendy but tasteful clothing for newborns through tweens. *454 Columbus Ave. (at 84th St.). www. greenstonesnyc.com.* ☎ *212/580-4322. AE, MC, V. Subway: B/C to 81st St.*

★★ **kids Playing Mantis** TRIBECA It sells "toys for life,"

beautiful creations crafted from natural materials: wood-carved forest-fairy houses, hand-hewn musical instruments, and other remarkable finds. *32 N. Moore St. (btw. Hudson and Varick sts.). www. friendlymantis.com.* ☎ *646/484-6845. Subway: 1 to Franklin St.*

★★ **kids Space Kiddets** FLAT IRON DISTRICT Toys and hip kids' wear—including dozens of patterned T-shirts and fancy jeans—sold by a friendly, helpful staff. Prices are on the high side, but tempered by frequent sales. *26 E. 22nd St. (btw. Broadway and Park Ave.). www.spacekiddets.com.* ☎ *212/420-9878. AE, MC. V. Subway: N/R to 23rd St.*

★★★ **kids Toy Tokyo** EAST VILLAGE Action figures, oddball board games, and hundreds of fist-sized or smaller toys (great stocking stuffers) are just a few of the temptations here. And yes, there are a ton of Japanese toys. *91 Second Ave. (btw. 5th and 6th sts.). www. toytokyo.com.* ☎ *212/673-5424. AE, MC, V. Subway: 6 to Astor Place.* ●

Action figures galore at Toy Tokyo.

Central Park

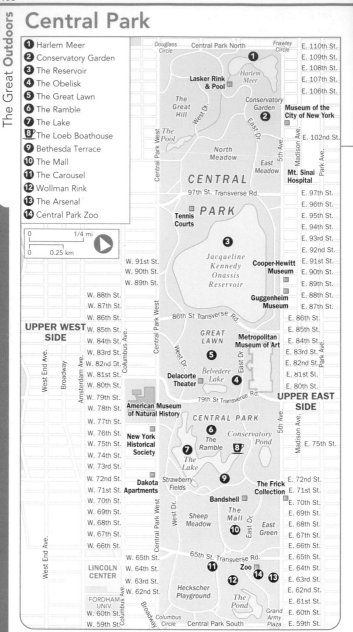

Previous page: Picnicking in Central Park.

Central Park serves as the city's backyard, its concert hall, its daytime pick-up bar, its outdoor gym, and, in summer, when dozens don bathing suits to soak up the rays, its green beach. The marvel of the park, beside its size (843 acres, a full 6% of Manhattan's total area), is the fact that none of it is "natural" in the usual sense. This park was created in the 1850s by landscape architects Frederick Law Olmstead and Calvert Vaux out of swampland, farms, and suburban towns. Every tree, every shrub, every lake, and most of the rolling hills were designed, planted, and blasted into existence by these two geniuses.

❶ Harlem Meer. This 11-acre *meer* (the Dutch word for lake) wasn't part of the original Central Park. Added in 1863, it has a natural, rugged shoreline and a community of swans. The **Charles A. Dana Discovery Center** (☎ 212/860-1370), on the northern shore, contains a year-round visitor center and hosts Central Park Conservancy seasonal exhibitions. *Fifth Ave. from 106th–110th sts.*

❷ ★★ Conservatory Garden. Commissioned by the WPA (Work Projects Administration) in 1936, this formal garden has many showpieces: an elegant Italian garden with a classical fountain, a mazelike English garden, a bronze statue of

The Secret Garden statue in the Conservatory Garden.

the children from the novel *The Secret Garden* in a reflecting water-lily pool. To reach the Reservoir (below) from here, walk south through the park or, to save a mile of walking, take a bus down Fifth Avenue to 86th Street. *Fifth Ave. and 105th St.*

❸ The Reservoir. Created in 1862 as part of the Croton Water System, the Reservoir was in use until 1994. Occupying 106 acres, it is surrounded by bridle and running paths. Many a celebrity and civilian has jogged along the 1.6-mile (2.6km) upper track, which overlooks the water and affords great skyline views. The reservoir holds a billion gallons of water and is 40 feet (12m) at its greatest depth, but these days it is only used as an emergency backup water supply. *Midpark from 85th–96th sts.*

❹ ★★ The Obelisk. This 71-foot (21m) artifact from Ancient Egypt was an 1881 gift to the U.S. from the khedive of Egypt. *See p 12.*

❺ ★ The Great Lawn. Expansive enough for simultaneous games of softball, volleyball, or soccer, the Great Lawn is also a plum spot for a picnic—especially on those warm summer nights when the New York Philharmonic or Metropolitan Opera performs for free (p 143). Bring along picnic fare from nearby gourmet grocery **Zabar's** (p 95). At the southern end,

A Word on Playgrounds

With a few exceptions, most of the park's playgrounds are located on the rim of the park, near the entrances. They pop up every 6 blocks or so. Adults are not supposed to enter them without children in tow.

★ **Belvedere Castle** (p 12) and its surrounding duck pond are particularly picturesque. *Midpark from 79th–85th sts.*

6 ★ **The Ramble.** Designed to mirror untamed nature, Olmstead called this 38-acre stretch his "wild garden." The Ramble has a seedy reputation after dark (I might not set foot in it after sunset), but during the day it's wonderful to explore. The inviting paths that curve through the wooded area offer some of the best scouting ground for bird-watchers in the city—some 230 species have been spotted here. A statue of a crouching cougar overlooks the East Drive between 76th and 77th streets. *Midpark from 73rd–79th sts.*

7 ★★ **The Lake.** By far the most beautiful body of water in the park, this idyllic lake was once a swamp.

On the Reservoir jogging path.

Rent a rowboat ($15 for the first hour) at the Loeb Boathouse (see below) and take your sweetie for a turn around the lake—the views from the water are superb. (At certain times of a year, a singing gondolier also plies the lake, but at $45/hour we're not sure it's worth the outlay). *Midpark from 71st–78th sts.*

8 ★ **The Loeb Boathouse.** At the eastern end of the Lake is the Loeb Boathouse, where you can rent boats and bikes as well as dine—and dine well. The upscale Lakeside Restaurant (lunch/brunch year-round; dinner Apr–Nov) is a lovely fine-dining space with alfresco lakeside seating under a white canopy. The menu is contemporary American. The casual Express Café serves breakfast, burgers, salads and sandwiches (year-round 8am–5pm daily). *Fifth Ave. (btw. 74th and 75th sts.).* www.thecentralparkboathouse.com. ☎ 212/517-2233. $–$$$.

9 ★★ **Bethesda Terrace.** The architectural heart of the park, this extraordinarily lovely area is filled with art. If you approach it from the Mall, you'll come to a ravishing carved gate, with symbols representing "day" and "night" (the witches on brooms). The fountain celebrates the opening of the Croton Aqueduct, which finally solved NYC's water problems in 1842. The *Angel Bethesda* was sculpted by Emma Stebbins, the first woman ever to receive this sort of commission from the city. *Midpark at 72nd St.*

🔟 ★★ **The Mall.** This beguiling promenade is shaded by a curving canopy of American elms—a favorite tree of the park's designers. At the south end of the Mall is the **Literary Walk,** flanked by statues of Shakespeare, Robert Burns, Sir Walter Scott, and other historic and literary figures. *Midpark from 66th–72nd sts.*

⓫ ★★ **kids** **The Carousel.** The original carousel was built in 1871; fires destroyed it and a successor. Park officials searched high and low for a replacement, only to discover this treasure abandoned in an old trolley building on Coney Island. Its 58 colorful steeds—among the largest carousel ponies in the world—were hand-carved by Russian immigrants Solomon Stein and Harry Goldstein in 1908. *Midpark at 64th St.* ☎ *212/439-6900, ext. 12. $3 ride. Apr–Oct daily 10am–6pm; Nov–Mar call.*

⓬ **kids** **Wollman Rink and Victorian Gardens Amusement Park.** Remember the flick *Love Story?* This is where he skated right before she died. In summer, the spot is home to the immaculate Victorian Gardens Amusement Park, geared toward young children. *Fifth Ave. (btw. 62nd and 63rd sts.). Hink. www.wollmanskatingrink. com,* ☎ *212/439-6900, Mon–Tues 10am–2:30pm, Wed–Thurs 10am–10pm, Fri–Sat 10am–11pm, Sun 10am–9pm. Admission $11–$17 adults, $6–$9 children 11 and under, skate rental $7. Victorian Gardens: www.victoriangardensnyc.com.* ☎ *212/982-2229. Daily 11am–7pm. Admission w/ unlimited rides $21.*

⓭ **The Arsenal.** Predating the park, this Gothic Revival building looks like a fortress—which it briefly was, when it lodged troops in the

Feeding the sheep at the Central Park Children's Zoo.

Civil War. It was later the original site of the American Museum of Natural History (p 50) and even home to some of P. T. Barnum's circus animals, from a black bear to white swans. Today, it holds the park headquarters and a third-floor art gallery. *Fifth Ave. and 64th St.* ☎ *311 in New York City or 212/NEW-YORK.*

⓮ ★★ **kids** **Central Park Zoo.** The Central Park Zoo was built in 1988 to replace a 1934 WPA-built structure that had become cramped and outdated. Today the zoo's 5½ acres house more than 400 animals. Watch sea lions cavorting in the Central Garden pool, polar bears splashing around their watery den, or penguins being fed in the chilly "Polar Circle". A favorite of all ages, the **Delacorte Clock,** a timepiece with six clockwork bronze animals twirl to music on the hour and half-hour. In the small **Tisch Children's Zoo,** kids can feed and pet tame farm animals. 🕐 *75 min. Fifth Ave. (btw. 63rd and 66th sts.). www.centralpark zoo.com.* ☎ *212/861-6030. Admission $18 adults, $15 seniors, $13 children 3–12, free for kids 2 and under. Daily 10am–4:30pm (extended hours for weekends, holidays, and spring/summer).*

The Great Outdoors

The **High Line**

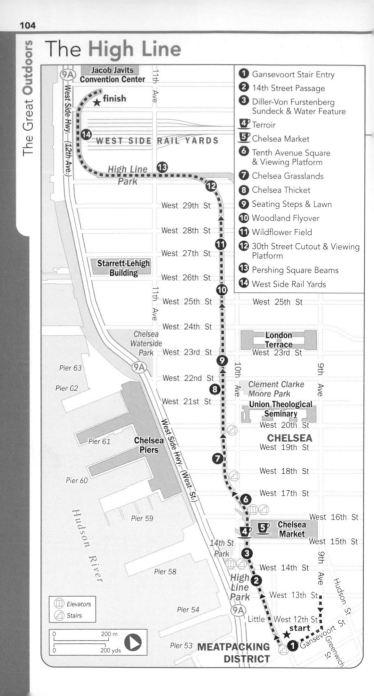

1. Gansevoort Stair Entry
2. 14th Street Passage
3. Diller-Von Furstenberg Sundeck & Water Feature
4. Terroir
5. Chelsea Market
6. Tenth Avenue Square & Viewing Platform
7. Chelsea Grasslands
8. Chelsea Thicket
9. Seating Steps & Lawn
10. Woodland Flyover
11. Wildflower Field
12. 30th Street Cutout & Viewing Platform
13. Pershing Square Beams
14. West Side Rail Yards

The High Line, an abandoned West Side elevated rail line, was smartly reinvented as an urban park, spawning imitators across the globe. Where freight trains once rumbled and later weeds grew wild, today a concrete pathway winds through a landscape of naturalistic plantings and public art installations, all with Hudson River views. Combine this tour with "Chelsea's Art & Architecture" (p 64) for a leisurely day.

Relaxing on the High Line.

❶ Gansevoort Stair Entry. The foliage in the **Gansevoort Woodland,** at the top of the stairs, changes with the seasons. In autumn, aromatic aster,

smokebush, and winterberry holly dust the paths in purple and red hues. In spring, walkways are pillowed in creamy white serviceberry blossoms. The old track's rusted rails are integrated into the landscaping. *Btw. Gansevoort and Little W. 12th sts.*

❷ ★★★ 14th Street Passage. You're walking through the only building that shares a support system with the original tracks. This was once a meat storage and packing facility; in fact, architects working on the High Line found sixty vats of animal carcasses in the basement here when they began their work. *At 14th St.*

❸ ★★★ Diller–Von Furstenberg Sundeck & Water Feature. Grab yourself a wooden chaise and admire the river views. Dip your toes in the scrim of water—a flattened waterfall, if you will—running the length of the sundeck. The bubbling almost drowns out the noise of the traffic. *Btw. 14th and 15th sts.*

Practical Matters

The High Line is open daily 7am to 11pm in summer (until 8pm in winter); admission is free. It's wheelchair-accessible, with elevators at 14th, 16th, 23rd and 30th streets, and has public restrooms at 16th. Keep in mind that the High Line's landscaping is at its loveliest in spring, summer, and fall.

4 & **5** ★★ **Terroir in warm weather, Chelsea Market in winter.** When the weather is nice, there are few more pleasant places to dine than the High Line's own wine bar cum restaurant. You'll find it at roughly 15th street. If it's not open, exit at 16th Street to find a former Nabisco factory, now Chelsea Market (at 75 Ninth Ave.), an excellent food market offering everything from gourmet hummus to some of the most creative tacos you'll ever try. *See p 117.*

6 ★ **Tenth Avenue Square & Viewing Platform.** Crowds flock to these tiered wooden bleachers plunked virtually on top of Tenth Avenue. You can stare down the traffic on Tenth through the big picture window—and the folks below can stare up. *At 17th St.*

7 ★ **Chelsea Grasslands.** Spring sees daffodils and hundreds of pink-and-white Lady Jane tulips. By late summer, prairie grasslands bend in the breeze. Take a seat on the wooden platforms for prime viewing all around. To the east, you'll spot the needle spire of the Empire State Building. To the west (btw. 18th and 19th sts.) is Frank Gehry's fanciful IAC office building (p 65). Across Eleventh Avenue is the Chelsea Piers sports complex (p 65), with a golf driving range atop a Hudson River pier. *Btw. 17th and 19th sts.*

8 ★ **Chelsea Thicket.** This dense planting of flowering shrubs and small trees includes hollies, winterberry, and redbud. *Btw. 20th and 21st sts.*

9 **Seating Steps & Lawn.** Here, where extra tracks once served as loading decks for adjacent warehouses, is a 4,900-square-foot swath of turf for sunbathing and picnicking. Stepped seating made of reclaimed teak anchors the southern end. At the northern end, a rise in the lawn lifts visitors above the walkway, with views of Brooklyn to the east and the Hudson River to the west. *Btw. 22nd and 23rd sts.*

What Was the High Line?

The railroad built America's Wild West, but it also helped build downtown Manhattan, where street-level freight trains chugged along the city's gritty West Side in the mid-1800s. Alas, as street traffic increased, Tenth Avenue became known as "Death Avenue" for its glut of gruesome accidents. Still, it wasn't until 1929 that the city did something about the problem, creating the West Side Improvement Project, which elevated miles of railroad track above the fray. The High Line opened in 1934, running from 34th Street to Spring Street. Eventually competition from trucking put it out of business, however, and in 1980 the last train still using the track was shut down. In 1999, the preservation of the old rail line entered the collective consciousness when the Friends of the High Line was founded by two neighborhood residents. Ten years later, the first section opened to the public. For more information, go to **www. thehighline.org**.

Strolling along the High Line's landscaped walkway.

⑩ ★★ Philip A. and Lisa Maria Falcone Flyover. A dense grove of tall shrubs and trees once grew between the tracks here when the trains stopped running. Today, a metal walkway rises 8 feet above the High Line's path, carrying visitors through a leafy sumac-and-magnolia tree line. *Btw. 25th and 26th sts.*

⑪ ★★ Wildflower Field. A landscape dominated by tough drought-resistant grasses and wildflowers took root on the High Line when trains stopped running. The modern-day landscape is planted not only with a variety of blooms, but also with many of the same native species that survived. *Btw. 26th and 29th sts.*

⑫ ★★ 30th Street Cutout & Viewing Platform. This viewing platform allows visitors to peer down through the grid of steel beams and girders to the traffic passing below on 30th Street. *At 30th St.*

⑬ ★★ Pershing Square Beams. What's a park without a playground? In this section over the rail yards, the viaduct's original beams were exposed and coated with rubber to create a jungle gym. It's open only to kids 12 and under and accompanying adults. *At 31st St.*

⑭ ★★★ West Side Rail Yards extension. In 2016, the final section of the High Line opened, and it's a beaut. This stretch makes a wide U because locomotives pulling heavy boxcars needed extra room to climb from street level up to the elevated tracks. It's a lovely part of the park, a little wilder than other areas. On one side you get views of the still working train tracks issuing out from Pennsylvania Station; on the other side you get the closest river views that the Highline affords. Until construction is complete on the major building projects at Hudson Yards (roughly 2020), this section will remain unlit, meaning it closes at sunset. *Btw. 31st and 34th sts.*

Green-Wood Cemetery

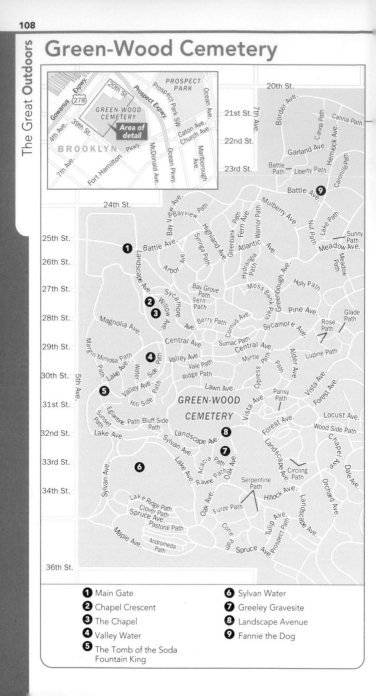

1 Main Gate
2 Chapel Crescent
3 The Chapel
4 Valley Water
5 The Tomb of the Soda Fountain King
6 Sylvan Water
7 Greeley Gravesite
8 Landscape Avenue
9 Fannie the Dog

"It is the ambition of the New Yorker to live upon Fifth Avenue, to take his airings in the Park, and to sleep with his fathers in Green-Wood." So declared the *New York Times* in 1866. Today, Brooklyn's 1838 Green-Wood Cemetery is a great place to revel in the outdoors, with 438 scenic acres and countless ornate mausoleums.

❶ ★★ **Main Gate.** Green-Wood has five entrances, but this Gothic gate with spires that stretch church-like into the sky is by far the most spectacular. A New York City Historic Landmark, it was built from 1861 to 1865 by architect Richard M. Upjohn. At the information booth inside, you can pick up a free map of the grounds. It lists the many famous (and infamous) residents—some 600,000 in all. These include Samuel Morse, Henry Ward Beecher, Leonard Bernstein, Boss Tweed, Nathaniel Currier and James Ives, Jean-Michel Basquiat, and hundreds of Civil War soldiers. A self-guided walking tour app is free. The cemetery also hosts excellent trolley tours. ⏲ *2 hr. 500 25th St. (at Fifth Ave.), Brooklyn. www.green-wood.com.* ☎ *718/768-7300. Daily 8am–5pm (extended hours in summer). Trolley tours $15–$20. Subway: N/R to 25th St. in Brooklyn.*

❷ ★ **Chapel Crescent.** Green-Wood's grand chapel (see below) is surrounded by stunning tombs. The B. Stephens tomb is shaped like a small Egyptian pyramid. The Chambettaz tomb has an angel statue overlooking the crescent as well as symbols from the secret society of the Freemasons.

❸ ★★★ **The Chapel.** A few minutes' walk from the main gates is Green-Wood's crowning glory. The 1911 chapel is a relatively recent arrival, its design inspired by Tom Tower at Oxford's Christ Church college, a 17th-century work by architect Christopher Wren. The multidomed structure is built entirely of Indiana limestone. The small interior frequently hosts readings and special exhibits that explore funerary art. Check **www.green-wood.com** for a calendar of events.

❹ **Valley Water.** Some of Green-Wood's ponds have been filled in to create new burial plots, but happily this stunning one remains. The avenue that curves around Valley Water is a treasure trove of 19th-century sculpture. Many of the monuments are partially draped by a carved "cloth." This popular Victorian Resurrectionist style reflected a belief that the body in the grave would rise on Judgment Day, when the cloth would fall away as if pulled back by the hand of God.

❺ ★ **The Tomb of the Soda Fountain King.** This towering work of sculpture is really just one giant tombstone: In 1870, it won the Mortuary Monument of the Year award. (Didn't know there was

A stately tomb in Green-Wood Cemetery.

Governor's Island, once a fort defending New York Harbor, now welcomes parkgoers.

such a thing, did you?) This is the resting place of John Matthews, the man who invented the soda fountain—and that information is about the only thing not carved into it. Gargoyles, members of the Matthews family, and Matthews himself are all here.

❻ Sylvan Water. The largest body of water in Green-Wood. Sylvan Water is surrounded by a series of tombs, some of which look large enough to house a (living) family.

❼ ★ Greeley Gravesite. Horace Greeley was an antislavery advocate who founded the *New York Tribune* and was a national figure. ("Go West, young man" is one of his famous aphorisms.) The views from his family plot are lovely.

❽ Landscape Avenue. This winding avenue offers memorable vistas and some great statuary.

❾ Fannie the Dog. Anyone who has ever loved a pet will relate to the engraving on the headstone of Fannie, sewing-machine inventor Elias Howe's pooch: "FROSTS OF WINTER NOR HEAT OF SUMMER / COULD MAKE HER FAIL IF MY FOOTSTEPS LED / AND MEMORY HOLDS IN ITS TREASURE CASKET / THE NAME OF MY DARLING WHO LIES DEAD." ●

Governors Island

A military base for 200 years, this 172-acre island—just a short (free) ferry ride from lower Manhattan—became a public park soon after being decommissioned in 1996. Visitors can explore the island's historic district, including a national monument centered around two 1812 fortresses. But most come to the beguiling automobile-free island for concerts, table-tennis championships, kite flying, views (improved in 2016 with the addition of little hills), and vintage amusement-park rides—or for a leisurely bike ride (BYO, or rent one for the day for $25). Info at ☎ 212/440-2200 or **www.govisland.com**. Ferries depart from Battery Maritime Building, Slip #7. Subway: 1 to South Ferry.

Dining Best Bets

Best Places for a Carnivore
Keens $$$ 72 W. 36th St. (p 123);
and Peter Luger $$$ 178 Broadway,
Brooklyn (p 125)

Best Vegetarian
Nix $$ 72 University Place (p 123)

Best French
Le Bernardin $$$$ 55 W. 51st St.
(p 123)

Best Cheap Eats
Great NY Noodletown $ 28 Bowery
(p 120)

Best Burger
Burger Joint $ 119 W. 56th St. (p 118)

Best Chinese
Mission Chinese $$ 171 E. Broadway
(p 124)

Best Party
Sammy's Famous Roumanian $$
157 Chrystie (p 125)

Best Fusion Cuisine
Momofuku Ssam Bar $$
207 Second Ave (p 124)

Best Delis
Barney Greengrass $ 541 Amster-
dam Ave. (p 117); and Katz's $
205 E. Houston St. (p 122)

Best Pizza
Keste $ 271 Bleecker St. (p 123)

Best Seafood
Le Bernardin $$$$ 55 W. 51st St.
(p 123)

Best Splurge
Eleven Madison Park $$$$
11 Madison Ave. (p 120)

Best Italian
Locanda Verde $$$ 377 Greenwich
St. (p 123)

Best New Restaurant
Mimi $$$ 185 Sullivan St. (p 23)

Best for Families
Gyu Kaku $ 321 W. 44th (p 121)

Restaurant Week: Prix-Fixe Dining

Everyone loves a deal, and Restaurant Week is one of New
York's best. It started more than a decade ago, when some of the
city's best dining spots began to offer three courses for a fixed low
price at lunch ($29) and dinner ($42). Now it's an institution that
lasts for several weeks in January and July/August. Check out **www.
opentable.com** or **www.nycvisit.com** for more info on participating
restaurants.

Previous page: Brasserie-style dining at Balthazar.

Downtown Dining

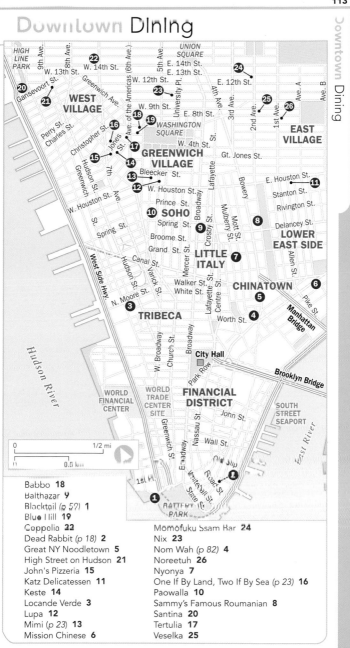

Babbo **18**
Balthazar **9**
Blacktail *(p 52)* **1**
Blue Hill **19**
Coppolia **22**
Dead Rabbit *(p 18)* **2**
Great NY Noodletown **5**
High Street on Hudson **21**
John's Pizzeria **15**
Katz Delicatessen **11**
Keste **14**
Locande Verde **3**
Lupa **12**
Mimi *(p 23)* **13**
Mission Chinese **6**
Momofuku Ssam Bar **24**
Nix **23**
Nom Wah *(p 82)* **4**
Noreetuh **26**
Nyonya **7**
One If By Land, Two If By Sea *(p 23)* **16**
Paowalla **10**
Sammy's Famous Roumanian **8**
Santina **20**
Tertulia **17**
Veselka **25**

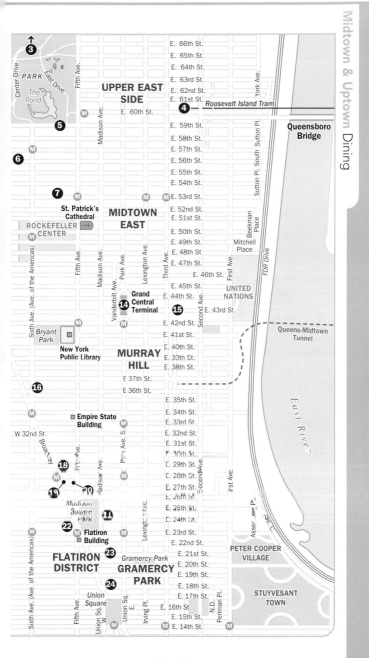

Restaurants A to Z

★★ **ABC Kitchen** UNION SQUARE *NEW AMERICAN* Chef Jean-Georges Vongerichten has taken on the farm-to-table trend with this rustic yet elegant spot uniquely located in a high-end furniture store (see p 96). Expect fresh, impeccably sourced ingredients and a delicious, impeccably prepared meal. Comfort food for foodies. *ABC Carpet & Home, 35 E. 18th St. (at Broadway). www.abc kitchennyc.com.* ☎ *212/475-5829. Main courses $21–$37. AE, DISC, MC, V. Lunch and dinner daily. Subway: 4/5/6/L/N/R to Union Sq.*

★ **Amy Ruth's** HARLEM *AMERICAN* The best soul food uptown—the chicken & waffles are topped with honey from an apiary on the roof. *113 W. 116th St. www. amyruthsharlem.com.* ☎ *212/280-8779. Main courses $10–$20. Breakfast, lunch, and dinner daily. Subway: 2, 3, B, C to 116th St.*

★★ **Babbo** WASHINGTON SQUARE *ITALIAN* A big star in celebrity chef Mario Batali's edible empire. Set in a warm, flower-filled town house, Babbo is lit from within with a special-occasion glow. The pasta-tasting menu is a smart

Special-occasion dining at Babbo.

choice. *110 Waverly Place (at Sixth Ave.). www.babbonyc.com.* ☎ *212/ 777-0303. Main courses $21–$32, 7-course tasting menus $95–$99. AE, MC, V. Dinner daily. Subway: A/C/E/ F/B/D to 4th St.*

★ **Balthazar** SOHO *FRENCH* The quintessential Parisian-style brasserie. Not only does Balthazar look picture-perfect, with its zinc bar, smoked mirrors, soaring ceiling, and serious, vest-wearing waiters, the food hits the mark as well. *80 Spring*

ABC Kitchen does farm-to-table food in rustic-chic style.

Foodie Food Halls

Forget Aunt Annie's pretzels. Gotham's food courts are dazzling displays, with food from pretty much every corner of the globe and almost every star chef in the city. My favorites include **Eataly** (see p 94), for Italian delights; and Grand Central Terminal's **Great Northern Food Hall** (p 8), which features scintillating Scandinavian fare. Other halls mix cuisines from different cultures, such as **Chelsea Market** (75 Ninth Ave. between 15th and 16th sts., Chelsea. www.chelseamarket.com), known for its hummus, halvah, Mexico City–style burritos, and Korean ramen; the swank **Plaza Food Hall** (in the Plaza Hotel, Fifth Ave. and Central Park South; the plazany.com), with its caviar bar, exquisite cakes, and hoity-toity tacos; and **City Kitchen,** just off Times Square. The latter gets crowded but has excellent Japanese noodles, gourmet donuts, and Persian sandwiches (it's at 700 Eighth Ave at 44th St., 2nd floor, http://citykitchen.rownyc.com). Kudos, too, to **The Pennsy** (at Pennsylvania Station, on 33rd and Seventh Ave., www.thepennsy.nyc); the near-Javits Center **City Market** (600 11th Ave. btw. 44th and 45th sts., www.gothamwestmarket.com); and **Smorgasburg** in Brooklyn (p 78), which is as much of a weekend event as it is a place to get grub.

St. (btw. Broadway and Crosby St.). www.balthazarny.com. ☎ 212/965-1414. Main courses $11–$43. Breakfast, lunch, dinner, and late-night dining. AE, DC, DISC, MC, V. Subway: 6 to Spring St, N/R to Prince St.

★ **Barney Greengrass** UPPER WEST SIDE *DELI* The Sturgeon King has been selling lox and bagels for a century at this favorite weekend brunch spot. The vintage counters and dairy case are beautiful. *541 Amsterdam Ave. (btw. 86th and 87th sts.). www.barneygreengrass.com.* ☎ *212/724-4707. Main courses $4.75–$22, smoked-fish platters $34–$56. AE, MC, V. Breakfast*

The Great Northern Food Hall in Grand Central Terminal.

and lunch (or brunch) Tues–Sun. Subway: 1/9 to 86th St.

★★★ Blue Hill GREENWICH VILLAGE *AMERICAN*

This soothing, understated Village townhouse space quietly goes about its business serving some of the most delicious food in town, with an admirable sustainable-foods philosophy that travels perfectly from purveyor to plate. Chef Dan Barber coaxes the best out of the best ingredients. Even lowly Brussels sprouts become irresistible. *75 Washington Place (btw. Sixth Ave. and Washington Sq. W.). www.blue hillfarm.com.* ☎ *212/539-1776. Tasting menu $88–$98. AE, DC, MC, V. Dinner daily. Subway: B/D/F/M/A/C/E to W. 4th St.*

★★ Boulud Sud UPPER WEST SIDE *MEDITERRANEAN*

The best place in the vicinity of Lincoln Center for a pre-performance meal, star chef Daniel Boulud's food is downright operatic, a masterful take on Mediterranean fare from the south of France to North Africa. And the room is elegant enough for your concert-going duds, too. *20 W. 64th. St (off Broadway.). www.boulud sud.com.* ☎ *212/595-1313. Main courses $32–$52. AE, DISC, MC, V.*

Chefs at Chelsea Market.

The Breslin.

Lunch and dinner daily until 11pm, brunch on weekends. Subway: 1 to 64th St.

★★ The Breslin FLATIRON DISTRICT *GASTROPUB*

All dark wood, beveled glass, and cozy niches, this is a warm oasis for gastronomes and homesick Brits. Meat is the star, from the celebrated lamb burger to the pork-belly platter to house-made sausage. Even the boiled peanuts are fried in pork fat. *Ace Hotel, 16 W. 29th St. (at Broadway). www.thebreslin.com.* ☎ *212/679-1939. Main courses $17–$36. AE, DC, DISC, MC, V. Breakfast, lunch and dinner Mon–Fri, brunch and dinner Sat–Sun. Subway: N/R to 28th St.*

★ Burger Joint MIDTOWN WEST *BURGERS*

Hidden behind a red curtain in the stylish lobby of Le Parker Meridien hotel, but far from a secret, lies a "joint" that might remind you of the greasy spoons of your college years. This one, however, far exceeds those with what

Sweets for the Sweet

When it comes to desserts, the Big Apple has definite polish. Here are just a few places where you can destroy your diet with glee. At Chinatown's **10 Below** (10 Mott St., near Canal St.; www.10belowicecream.com; no phone) Thai ice cream is created right before your eyes. In the East Village, **Chikalicious** (203 E. 10th St., off Second Ave.; www.chikalicious.com; ☎ 212/995-9511) is a dessert-only restaurant where all customers get a marvelous three-course tasting menu for $16, while nearby **Venieros** (342 E. 11th St. at First Ave.; www.venierospastry.com; ☎ 212/674-7070) is a beloved Italian bakery that's been in business since 1894. SoHo's **Dominique Ansel** (189 Spring St., between Thompson and Sullivan sts.; www.dominqueansel.com; ☎ 212/219-2773) sells not just Ansel's famous "cronuts," but also wonderful and very French pastries of all sorts. A few blocks east, **Rice to Riches** (37 Spring St., between Mott and Mulberry sts.; www.ricetoriches.com; ☎ 212/274-0008) is a delightful one-trick pony—it serves only rice pudding, but tarted up with all sorts of exotic flavorings. The Upper East Side's **Lady M Cake Boutique** (41 E. 78th St. near Madison Ave.; www.ladym.com; ☎ 212/452-2222) whips up crepe cakes to die for.

may be the best burgers in the city. Even better, the prices are more in keeping with a greasy spoon than a hotel of Le Parker Meridien's caliber. *119 W. 56th St. (btw. Sixth and Seventh aves.). www.parkermeridien. com.* ☎ *212/708-7414. Burgers $9–$10. Cash only. Lunch and dinner daily. Subway: F/N/Q/R to 57th St.*

★ **Coppelia** CHELSEA *LATIN AMERICAN* Diner-like on the outside, inside is another world. Coppelia's soundtrack is salsa, its decor is tropical, and the menu ranges across the Caribbean and Latin America, offering up perfect renditions of such regional faves as *lomo saltado* (Peruvian tomato and ginger beef stir-fry), Cuban roast pork with *chicharons*, and Brazilian sweet-corn *empanadas*. *207 W. 14th St. (near Seventh Ave.). www. ybandco.com.* ☎ *212/858-5001. Main courses $7–$18. AE, DC, DISC,*

MC, V. Daily 24 hr. Subway: 1/2/3 to 14th St.

★★★ **Cosme** MIDTOWN EAST *MEXICAN* Cosme is the first U.S. restaurant from Enrique Olvera, owner of Mexico City's iconic Pujol Restaurant (named 20th best restaurant in the world by the Diner's Club Academy). It brings to New York the kind of contemporary, deeply luxurious Mexican food that it had yet to experience. *Tip:* If you can't get a reservation, go anyway. There's a lot of seating for walk-ins at the front. *35 E. 21st St (btw. Broadway and Park Ave. South). www.cosmenyc.com.* ☎ *212/913-9659. Main courses $28–$59. AE, DC, DISC, MC, V. Lunch and dinner daily. Subway: 6/N/R to 23rd St.*

★★ **Danji** THEATER DISTRICT *KOREAN* Danji reinvents Korean classics in odd but very tasty ways.

Eleven Madison Park.

That might mean a kimchee, bacon, and Spam paella, or tofu infused with ginger before being flash-fried. Young chef Hooni Kim got his chops cooking for such master chefs as Daniel Boulud. Warning: the flavors are big here, but the space is tiny, so you *will* get to know your neighbor. *346 W. 52nd St. (btw. Eighth and Ninth aves.). www.danjinyc.com.* ☎ *212/586-2880. Main courses $13–$26, with most in the teens. AE, MC, V. Lunch and dinner Mon–Sat. Subway: C/E to 50th St.*

★★ Dominick's THE BRONX
ITALIAN The dining room is small and slightly cramped. You may have a long wait for a table on weekend evenings. But hang in and you'll be well taken care of by the skilled if taciturn waitstaff at this legendary spot, which has no menus and no checks. You want some clams to start? A salad or a stuffed artichoke maybe? Yes, yes, and yes. Follow with a sampling of perfect seafood pastas, buttery shrimp *franchese*, and a perfectly cooked steak. *2335 Arthur Ave. (btw. 187th St. and Crescent Ave.).* ☎ *718/733-2807. Main courses $10–$25. Cash only. Lunch and dinner Wed–Mon. Subway: B/D to 183rd St.*

★★★ Eleven Madison Park
FLATIRON DISTRICT *AMERICAN*
Chef Daniel Humm has won every award in the book (including a James Beard award—the culinary world's Oscar—for best restaurant in the U.S.A.) Exquisite tasting menus are served in a soaring Art Deco space, with two-story windows overlooking Madison Square Park. After the meal, each guest is treated to a tour of the kitchen. *11 Madison Ave. (at 24th St.). www.eleven madisonpark.com.* ☎ *212/889-0905. Tasting menu $195. AE, DC, DISC, MC, V. Lunch Mon–Sat, dinner daily. Subway: N/R/6 to 23rd St.*

Gray's Papaya UPPER WEST SIDE
HOT DOGS Unless you are heading to Coney Island for an original **Nathan's** hot dog, Gray's Papaya serves the best—and cheapest—dogs in the city. Open 24 hours, the Gray's outpost on the Upper West Side is an institution. *2090 Broadway (at 72nd St.).* ☎ *212/799-0243. Hot dog $1.95. Cash only. Subway: 1/2/3 to 72nd St.*

★★ Great NY Noodletown
CHINATOWN *CHINESE* Don't be fooled by the run-down diner appearance; the food here may be the best in Chinatown. The

Gray's Papaya, a cheap-eats classic.

High Street on Hudson.

seafood-based noodle soups are spectacular, the salt-baked shrimp is as good as you'll find anywhere, and the platters of roast pig, roast pork (yes, there is a difference), and spareribs on rice are irresistible. Whatever you order is very easy on the wallet, adding to Noodletown's immense appeal. *28 Bowery (at Bayard St.). www.greatny noodletown.com.* ☎ *212/349-0923. Platters/soups $6–$16. Cash only. Breakfast, lunch, and dinner daily. Subway: N/R/6 to Canal St.*

★ kids **Gyu Kaku** THEATER DISTRICT *JAPANESE BBQ* Think Benihana but with *you* as the chef. Diners choose proteins and veggies, and then cook them themselves on a sizzling metal tabletop, dipping them in three splendid sauces. It's great fun, delicious, and kids love it. *321 W. 44th St. (btw. Eighth and Ninth aves.). www.gyu-kaku.com.* ☎ *646/892-9113. Average meal $17–$21. Lunch and dinner daily. Subway: A/C/E to 42nd St.*

★★ **High Street on Hudson** GREENWICH VILLAGE *AMERICAN* Paleo dieters beware: you'll be sorely tested here. The linchpins of the menu are breads and they are divine, crafted from locally milled flour and non-commercial yeasts. The grain-a-palooza also includes a range of fabulous pastas and, often, sauces with the added crunch of soured oats (a perfect accompaniment to the tender roast Long Island duck). A casually wonderful resto. *637 Hudson St. (at Horatio St.). www.highstreeton hudson.com* ☎ *917/388-3944. Main courses $12–$28. Daily breakfast, lunch and dinner. Subway: A/C/ E/ L to 14th St.–8th Ave.*

★★★ **ilili Restaurant** MIDTOWN EAST *LEBANESE* A ravishing, Escher-like jumble of wooden squares climb the walls of this restaurant, all the way up to the cathedral-height ceilings. That complexity also marks the food, which is sophisticated and surprising, whether you're digging into a plate of musky chicken livers cut by a tart tamarind syrup, or tasting one of the traditional spreads, which take the usual hummus and baba ganoush to another level. *236 Fifth Ave. (at 28th St.). www.ililinyc.com.* ☎ *646/683-2929. Average meals $26–$32. Lunch and dinner daily. AE, MC, V. Subway: N/R to 28th St.*

★★★ **Ippudo** MIDTOWN WEST *JAPANESE* Ramen can be life-changing. That may sound hyperbolic, but try the silky soups here, made from the finest Berkshire pork and filled with toothsome noodles,

Ramen at Ippudo.

and you'll see I'm right. Ippudo's only drawback? I'm not the only one who feels this way, so the lines to get in can be epic (no reservations). Also at 65 Fourth Ave. *321 West 51st St (btw. Eighth and Ninth Aves). www.ippudony.com.* ☎ *212/ 974-2500. Main courses $15–$18. AE,MC, V. Lunch and dinner daily. Subway: C/E to 51st St.*

★ **Jacob's Pickles** UPPER WEST SIDE *AMERICAN* Pickles, pick-ups, and artisanal beers: Those are the holy trinity at this buzzy tavern. It's become THE place for the neighborhood's singles, who scope one another out over some of the finest comfort food in town, like fried chicken atop huge, flaky bis-cuits, and creamy grits with head-on shrimp. *509 Amsterdam Ave. (btw. 84th and 85th sts.). www.jacobs pickles.com.* ☎ *212/470-5566. Brunch (starting at 10am) through late night daily. Subway: 1, B, C to 86th St.*

kids John's Pizzeria of Bleecker Street GREENWICH VILLAGE *PIZZA* The decor in this longtime Bleecker Street favorite, founded in 1929, hasn't changed over the years: wooden booths, Olde Italy mural, and tin ceilings. The pizza hasn't changed, either. The brick-oven pies are thin, crispy, and delicious. There's also a branch in Times Square (260 W. 44th St ;

☎ 212/391-7560). *278 Bleecker St. (btw. Sixth and Seventh aves.). www. johnsbrickovenpizza.com.* ☎ *212/243-1680. Pizzas $12–$14, toppings $2. No credit cards. Lunch and dinner daily. Subway: A/C/E/B/D/F/M at W. 4th St.*

★ **Katz's Delicatessen** LOWER EAST SIDE *DELI* Founded in 1888, this homely, cacophonous space is one of the city's last great old-time delis. No one makes a better pas-trami sandwich. Plus, you can see the spot where Meg Ryan per-formed her famous scene in *When Harry Met Sally*. *205 E. Houston St. (at Ludlow St.). www.katzdeli.com.* ☎ *212/254-2246. Sandwiches $3–$10, other items $5–$18. AE, MC,*

Katz's Deli.

V. Breakfast, lunch, and dinner daily. Subway: F to Second Ave.

★★★ Keens MIDTOWN WEST

STEAK If you're searching for olde New York, look no further than this 1885 survivor tucked away on a side street near Madison Square Garden. The space has always been wonderful; now the food is its equal. I had one of the best steaks I've ever eaten here. *72 W. 36th St. (at Sixth Ave.). www.keens.com.* ☎ *212/947-3636. Main courses $28–$64. AE, DC, DISC, MC, V. Lunch & dinner Mon–Fri, dinner Sat and Sun. Subway: 1/2/3/9 to 34th St./Penn Station.*

★★★ Keste GREENWICH

VILLAGE *PIZZA* Invading John's Pizzeria's Bleecker Street turf, Neapolitan upstart Keste offers artisanal pizza following the strict guidelines of the Association of Neapolitan Pizza. This means the chefs use only the best ingredients for the more than 40 different creations—the worst thing about Keste is choosing your pie. *271 Bleecker St. (btw. Seventh Ave. and Carmine St.). www.kestepizzeria.com.* ☎ *212/243-1500. Pizza (entire pies only) $9–$26. AE, MC, V. Lunch and dinner daily. Subway: A/B/C/D/E/F/M to W. 4th St.*

★★★ Le Bernardin MIDTOWN

WEST*FRENCH/SEAFOOD* Chef Eric Ripert is a giant on the NYC culinary scene and a master with seafood. The formal service is impeccable. *55 W. 51st St. (btw. Sixth and Seventh aves.). www.le-bernardin.com.* ☎ *212/489-1515. Prix fixe dinner $150, tasting menu $220. AE, DC, DISC, MC, V. Lunch Mon–Fri, dinner Mon–Sat. Subway: N/R to 49th St.; 1/9 to 50th St.*

★★ Locanda Verde TRIBECA

ITALIAN Chef Andrew Carmellini became a celebrity chef after opening Locanda Verde—and for good reason. Here, he brings a culinary master's touch to simple, rustic Italian fare. This eatery—located in The Greenwich Hotel (p 159)—is popular, so book early. The sheep's-milk ricotta sprinkled with sea salt and herbs slathered on crostini will make any reservation hassles quickly fade away. *377 Greenwich St. (at N. Moore St.). www.locandaverdenyc.com.* ☎ *212/925-3797. Main courses $24–$38. AE, DISC, MC, V. Breakfast, lunch, and dinner daily. Subway: 1 to Franklin St.*

★ Lupa GREENWICH VILLAGE

ITALIAN This brick-lined homage to a Roman trattoria has been filled to capacity since it opened. The food is impeccable and often inventive, and the prices won't bankrupt you. It's part of the Batali/Bastianich empire. *170 Thompson St. (btw. Houston and Bleecker sts.). www.luparestaurant.com.* ☎ *212/982-5089. Main courses $13–$28. AE, MC, V. Lunch and dinner daily. Subway: B/D/F/M/A/C/E to W. 4th St.*

★★ Nix GREENWICH VILLAGE

VEGETARIAN And what is "nixed" here is meat. But this newbie's chefs cook in such a happily indulgent fashion—cream and butter and cheese, oh my!—even dedicated flesh-eaters leave satisfied.

Lupa Restaurant.

New York's Pizza Universe

In my biased but expert opinion, there is no better town for pizza west of Naples than New York. A pizza place can be found on almost every city block, but I will be the first to admit that many of them aren't worth the $3 advertised for a slice. While in New York, stick to the standouts, of which there are many. Downtown has the great slice joint **Joe's Pizza ★★** (7 Carmine St., at Bleecker St.; ☎ 212/255-3946). Frank Sinatra had pies from the wonderful old-school **Patsy's Pizzeria** (2287 First Ave., btw. 117th and 118th sts., East Harlem; ☎ 212/534-9783) shipped to Las Vegas. If you don't feel like a Nathan's hot dog at Coney Island, head to **Totonno's Pizzeria Napolitano ★★** (1524 Neptune Ave., btw. W. 15th and W. 16th sts., Coney Island, Brooklyn; ☎ 718/372-8606), where the coal-fired oven has been churning out crispy charred-crust pizzas since 1924. In the Bronx's Little Italy on Arthur Ave., **Trattoria Zero Otto Nove ★** (2357 Arthur Ave., at 186th St.; ☎ 718/220-1027) features innovative pizzas like butternut-squash puree with smoked mozzarella, made in a wood-burning brick oven. I also highly recommend the pizza at **John's** (p 122) and **Keste ★★★** (p 123).

72 University Place (btw. 9th and 10th sts.). www.nixny.com. ☎ 212/498-9393. Main courses $12–$19. AE, MC, V. Daily 5–11pm. Subway: 4/5/6/N/Q/R/L to Union Sq.

★★★ Mission Chinese LOWER EAST SIDE *CHINESE* Groovy décor, groovy cocktails, and some of the grooviest (and spiciest) food in the city—this is NOT your typical take-out Chinese joint. Be sure to challenge your tastebuds with the fiery *kung pao pastrami* and the signature thrice-cooked bacon with Shanghai rice cakes. Great for groups (who doesn't love tables with a lazy Susan in the center?). 171 E. Broadway (near Rutgers St.). www.mcfny.com. ☎ 212/432-0300. Main courses $13–$37. Dinner daily, dim sum brunch weekends. Subway: F to East Broadway.

★★ The Modern MIDTOWN WEST *AMERICAN* Dining in this elegant space overlooking MoMA's sculpture garden makes you feel as if you're at the center of a very sophisticated urban universe—and you are. The food lives up to the setting, and the cross-section of New Yorkers crisply doing business makes this a great spot to see the local tribe in action. *The Museum of Modern Art, 9 W. 53rd St. (btw. Fifth and Sixth aves.). www.themodernnyc. com. ☎ 212/333-1220. 3-course prix-fixe menu $118, 6-course tasting menu $158. AE, DC, DISC, MC, V. Lunch Mon–Fri, dinner Mon–Sat. Subway: E/M to Fifth Ave./53rd St.*

★★★ Momofuku Ssam Bar UNION SQUARE *ASIAN FUSION* Chef/owner/culinary savant David Chang pays homage to pork in many, many forms here. There's the delightful Asian-style burrito the restaurant is named after; the artisanal ham plate; and the pièce de résistance, a whole pork butt for 6 to 10 people (advance orders required). Beyond pig, Chang is a whiz with vegetables and fish

Black crab and fried green tomatoes at Paowalla.

and . . . well, everything he serves in this loud and casual temple of gastronomy. *207 Second Ave. (at 13th St.).* www.momofuku.com. ☎ *212/777-7773. Main courses $10–$29. Daily lunch and dinner. Subway: N/Q/R/ L/4/5/6 to Union Sq.*

★★ Noreetuh EAST VILLAGE
HAWAIIAN This little-known cuisine is given the gourmet treatment by a rising young chef with real gastronomic chops. And yes, spam is part of some dishes. *128 First Ave. (btw. 7th St. and St. Marks Pl.).* www. noreetuh.com. ☎ *646/892-3050. Main courses $17–$25. Tues–Sun dinner, brunch weekends. Subway: 6 to Astor Place or L to First Ave.*

★ Nyonya LITTLE ITALY
MALAYSIAN Spacious, bustling, and inexpensive, Nyonya introduces diners to this wonderfully varied cuisine. Try the *roti canai* (a pancake with a curry chicken dipping sauce). *199 Grand St. (btw. Mulberry and Mott sts.).* www.ilove nyonya.com. ☎ *212/619-0085. Main courses $6–$23. No credit cards. Lunch and dinner daily. Subway: 6 to Spring St.*

★★ Paowalla SOHO INDIAN
Top Chef winner Floyd Cardozo's breezy but accomplished new restaurant is a showplace for both the chef's vibrant imagination and his deep knowledge of Indian traditions. The name means "bread maker" and those are superb (cooked in a coal-fired pizza oven left by previous tenants), but so is the entire menu, ranging from subtly spiced tureens of baked crab to fiery pork ribs *vindaloo. 195 Spring St. (at Sullivan St.)* www.paowalla. com. ☎ *212/235-1098. Dishes $7–$29. Dinner daily, brunch on weekends. Subway: C/E to Spring St., 1 to Houston.*

★★★ Peter Luger Steakhouse
BROOKLYN *STEAK* This Brooklyn institution is porterhouse heaven. The meat cuts like butter, and the waiters are properly crusty. *178 Broadway (at Driggs Ave.), Brooklyn.* www.peterluger.com. ☎ *718/387-7400. Main courses $25–$55. Debit cards and checks with ID accepted. Lunch and dinner daily. Subway: J/M/Z to Marcy Ave.*

Sammy's Famous Roumanian Restaurant LOWER EAST SIDE
ROUMANIAN A raucous bar mitzvah masquerading as a restaurant.

Peter Luger Steakhouse, Brooklyn's famous old-school meatery.

You go to this basement restaurant to eat chopped liver drowning in *schmaltz* (liquefied chicken fat), do shots from a bottle of vodka encased in ice, and sing along to the goofball on the electric piano, who plays tunes from *Fiddler on the Roof* and tells the hoariest jokes imaginable. And you know what? You'll have the time of your life. An only-in-NYC kind of joint. *157 Chrystie St. (at Delancey St.). www.sammysromanian.com. ☎ 212/673-0330. Main dishes average $22–$37. Tues–Sun dinner only. Subway: F to Delancey St., B/D/Q to Grand St.*

★★ Santina MEATPACKING DISTRICT *MEDITERRANEAN* This exuberant restaurant, with its sherbet-colored chandeliers and indoor palm trees, is set in a glass cube under the High Line. Specialties include *ceccina* (chickpea-flour pancakes with savory toppings) and an array of shellfish dishes. *820 Washington St. (at Gansevoorte St.). www.santinanyc.com. ☎ 212/254-3000. Main courses $19–$30. Daily 10am–midnight. Subway: A/C/L to 14th St.*

★★★ Sushi Yasuda MIDTOWN EAST *JAPANESE* Pure Japanese sushi, as it's been made for centuries (that is, no mayonnaise or other fusion touches), cut, dabbed with soy sauce, and patted into shape by master chefs. That's the zen formula here, and it can't be improved on. *Tip:* Go for the nigiri sushi rather than rolls; with fish this meltingly tender, you don't want it buried in a lot of rice. *204 E. 43rd St. (btw. Second and Third aves.). www.sushiyasuda.com. ☎ 212/972-2001. Sushi $5–$15 per piece, including gratuities. AE, MC, V. Lunch and dinner Mon–Sat. Subway: 4/5/6/7/S to 42nd St.–Grand Central.*

Tertulia, a Spanish taberna transplanted to Greenwich Village.

★★ Tertulia GREENWICH VILLAGE *SPANISH* At this quintessential Iberian taberna, the food is cooked (mostly) in a roaring, wood-fired oven in the back, copied from one the chef saw in a small Basque town. The variety of tapas is astonishing, the paella has just the right crusty crunch. *359 6th Ave. (at Washington St.). www.tertulianyc.com. ☎ 646/559-9909. Tapas $6–$12; paella (for several people) $45. Lunch and dinner daily. Subway: A/B/C/D/E/F to West 4th St.*

Veselka EAST VILLAGE *UKRANIAN* When Veselka debuted in 1954, this neighborhood was awash in Ukrainian diners (and Ukrainians). As the area changed, the eateries disappeared, leaving this crowded, friendly place as the standard-bearer for borscht, pierogi, kielbasa, and other Eastern European staples. *144 Second Ave. (at 9th St.). www.veselka.com. ☎ 212/228-9682. Main courses $10–$17. Daily 24 hr. Subway: 6 to Astor Place.* ●

Nightlife **Best Bets**

Best **Old-School Atmosphere**
King Cole Bar, *2 E. 55th St. (p 134)*

Best **Fake Old-School Atmosphere**
The Dead Rabbit, *30 Water St. (p 18)*

Best **Choice of Single-Malt Scotches**
d.b.a., *41 First Ave. (p 132)*

Best **Place to Bowl & Sip a Martini**
Bowlmor Times Square, *229 W. 44th St. (p 132)*

Best **Cocktails**
Pegu Club, *77 W. Houston St. (p 134)*

Best **Hotel Bar**
Bemelmans Bar, *The Carlyle, 35 E. 76th St. (p 132)*

Best **Museum Bar**
Roof Garden, *Metropolitan Museum of Art, 1000 Fifth Ave. (p 134)*

Best **Vodka Selection**
Russian Samovar, *256 W. 52nd St. (p 135)*

Best **Bar with a View**
Roof Garden, *Metropolitan Museum of Art, 1000 Fifth Ave. (p 134)*

Best **Bar for Hearing the Written Word**
KGB Bar, *85 E. 4th St. (p 133)*

Take the L Train: Billyburg Bars

Just over the bridge in Brooklyn, Williamsburg is an arts and nightlife hub (see p 76 for more on the 'hood). To check out some of the city's freshest bars and clubs, you only need to take a short ride on the L train from 14th Street in Manhattan to Lorimer Street in Brooklyn. **Union Pool** (www.union-pool.com) is a welcoming bar with a large outdoor space, velvet lounges, and a post-hipster crowd. **Pete's Candy Store** (www.petescandystore.com) is a nifty tavern with live music, trivia, spelling-bee nights, and a Sunday backyard barbecue. If you want to see a hot band in a top-notch setting, the **Music Hall of Williamsburg** (www.musichallof williamsburg.com)—a sister club to the Bowery Ballroom and Mercury Lounge in Manhattan—is a good bet. Also hit **The Shanty** (p 77) and **Maison Premier** (p 79).

Previous page: Bartender at Bemelman's Bar in the Carlyle Hotel.

Downtown Nightlife

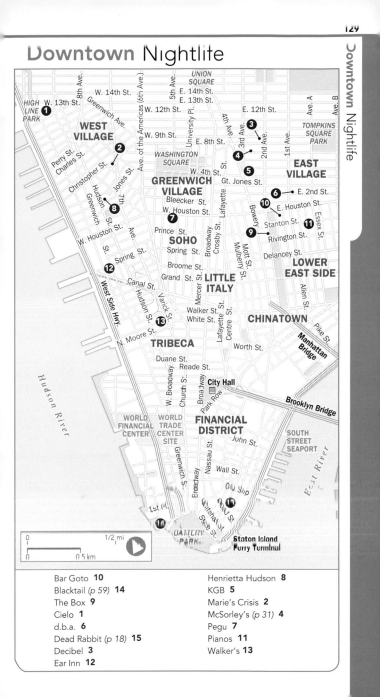

Bar Goto **10**
Blacktail *(p 59)* **14**
The Box **9**
Cielo **1**
d.b.a. **6**
Dead Rabbit *(p 18)* **15**
Decibel **3**
Ear Inn **12**

Henrietta Hudson **8**
KGB **5**
Marie's Crisis **2**
McSorley's *(p 31)* **4**
Pegu **7**
Pianos **11**
Walker's **13**

Midtown & Uptown Nightlife

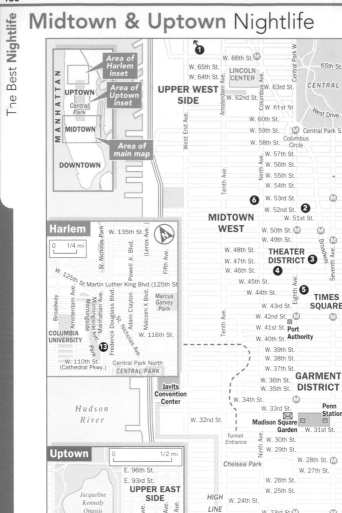

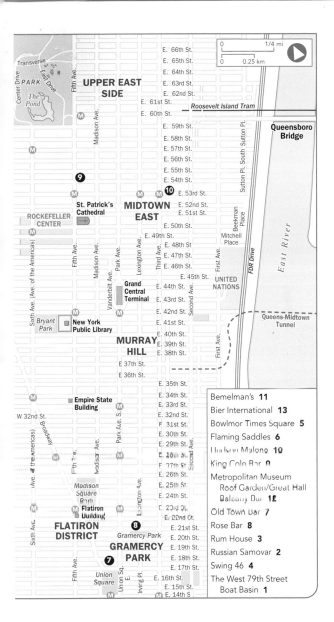

Bemelman's **11**

Bier International **13**

Bowlmor Times Square **5**

Flaming Saddles **6**

Hudson Malone **10**

King Cole Bar **9**

Metropolitan Museum
Roof Garden/Great Hall
Balcony Bar **12**

Old Town Bar **7**

Rose Bar **8**

Rum House **3**

Russian Samovar **2**

Swing 46 **4**

The West 79th Street
Boat Basin **1**

Nightlife A to Z

Bars & Cocktail Lounges
★★★ Bar Goto LOWER EAST SIDE Named for owner Kenta Goto, formerly of the iconic Pegu Club (p 134), this sophisticated drinkery puts a Japanese spin on its décor, cocktails, and snacks. That might mean liquors mixed with green tea powder, miso, or even a topping of marshmallow. All is served in a woodsy, square room that wouldn't be out of place in Kyoto. *245 Eldridge St. (near E. Houston).www.bargoto.com. ☎ 212/475-4411. Subway: F to Second Ave.*

★★ Bemelmans Bar UPPER EAST SIDE A playful mural by illustrator Ludwig Bemelmans, author of the *Madeline* children's books, decorates this old-school white-gloved lounge in the Carlyle hotel. Perched at one of the tables set around a piano that tinkles with show standards, you might even forget to check your cell phone while sipping perfectly made classic cocktails. *35 E. 76th St. (at Madison Ave.). ☎ 212/744-1600. Subway: 6 to 77th St.*

★ Bier International HARLEM Take the word "International" seriously. This buzzy nightspot has 18 international drafts and 20 bottled beers from all over the globe. It's all served in an airy, industrial-chic space with breeze-catching tables on the sidewalk outside. *2099 Frederick Douglass Blvd. (btw. 113th and 114th sts.). www.bierinternational. com. ☎ 212/876-8838. Subway: B/C to Cathedral Pkwy./110th St.*

Bowlmor Times Square TIMES SQUARE This 90,000-square-foot mega-entertainment complex in Times Square has 50 bowling lanes in seven New York–themed sections, splashy carnival games, and an epic sports bar with stadium seating. *Times Square Building, 229 W. 44th St. (btw. Seventh and Eighth aves.). www.bowlmor.com. ☎ 212/680-0012. Subway: R/S/W/1/2/3/7 to 42nd St./Times Sq.*

The Box LOWER EAST SIDE NYC nightlife at its raunchiest, the Box is a Belle Epoque–styled bar/theater, with a millennium mentality. Guests arrive around midnight for drinking, dancing, and mingling; a burlesque show starts at 1am, always featuring topless dancers and usually some kind of oddball magician, acrobat, transsexual performer, or comedian. It can be fun, though it's often X-rated. *189 Chrystie St. (btw. Stanton and Rivington sts.). www.theboxnyc.com. ☎ 212/982-9301. Subway: F to Second Ave.*

★ d.b.a. EAST VILLAGE Lounges dominate the city, but dba is a refreshing change of pace. It's an

Carnival at Bowlmor Lanes.

Behind the bar at d.b.a.

unpretentious neighborhood bar—a beer- or whiskey-lover's dream. The collection of single-malt scotches is phenomenal. *41 First Ave. (btw. 2nd and 3rd sts.).* ☎ *212/475-5097. Subway: F to Second Ave.*

★ **Decibel** EAST VILLAGE   A gritty, underground sake bar, Decibel is a center of social life for many of the ex-pat Japanese living in NYC. In fact, most of the clientele are Japanese, the soundtrack is Japanese rock, and the bar food can be exotic (dried squid, anyone?). *240 E 9th St. (btw. Second and Third aves.).* www.sakebar decibel.com ☎ *212/979-2733. Subway: 6 to Astor Place.*

★★★ **Ear Inn** SOHO   The Ear Inn is set in one of the oldest buildings on Manhattan: a gable-roofed, two-story Federal townhouse built by African American Revolutionary War hero James Brown in 1817. It got its current name when the "B" on the neon sign outside went on the fritz. Today, this mini-museum of a bar (there's historical ephemera everywhere) is popular with a wide range of New Yorkers, from 20-something gallery hoppers to 50-something motorcycle enthusiasts. *326 Spring St. (near Greenwich St.).* www.earinn.com. ☎ *212/226-9020. Subway: 1 to Canal St., C/E to Spring St.*

★★ **Hudson Malone** MIDTOWN EAST   A real New York "joint" (tin ceilings, brass rail at the bar, photos of famous customers on the walls) that may well be the friendliest pub in town. Also one of the best at mixology: I dare you to find a drier martini anywhere. *218 E. 53rd St. (off Third Ave.).* www.hudson malone.com ☎ *212/355-6607. Subway: E/M to 53rd St. or 6 to 51st.*

KGB Bar EAST VILLAGE   Formerly a Ukrainian social club, this 2nd-floor bar decorated in Communist memorabilia is now a mecca for some of the city's best author readings, be it fiction, nonfiction, or poetry. There's never a cover, and the drinks are more than affordable. *85 E. 4th St. (btw. Second and Third aves.).* ☎ *212/505-3360. Subway: 6 to Astor Place.*

Bellying up to the King Cole Bar.

★★ King Cole Bar MIDTOWN EAST   The Bloody Mary was born here, in the tony St. Regis Hotel. The Maxfield Parrish mural alone is worth the price of a classic cocktail (but egads, what a price!). It's a small but memorable spot. *2 E. 55th St. (at Fifth Ave.). www.king colebar.com. ☎ 212/744-4300. Subway: E to Fifth Ave./53rd St.*

★★ Metropolitan Museum Roof Garden/Great Hall Balcony Bar UPPER EAST SIDE   Every Friday and Saturday night from 4 to 8:30pm, the mezzanine level of the Met's lobby transforms into a lounge with live classical music. When the weather warms, take the elevator up to the **Roof Garden** for drinks with sumptuous views of the park. *Metropolitan Museum of Art, 1000 Fifth Ave. (at 82nd St.). www.metmuseum.org. ☎ 212/535-7710. Subway: 4/5/6 to 86th St.*

Old Town Bar FLATIRON DISTRICT   You know a bar is old when the burgers and fries are shuttled from the kitchen via dumb-waiter. This place was immortalized by David Letterman in the opening credits of his late-night show but has been around a lot longer than Dave. It's a hangout for the literary set, but you don't have to be a wordsmith to enjoy a beer here. *45 E. 18th St. (btw. Broadway and Park Ave. S.). www.oldtownbar.com. ☎ 212/529-6713. Subway: 4/5/6/ L/N/R/Q to 14th St./Union Sq.*

★★ Pegu Club SOHO   Self-described "gatekeepers of classic cocktail culture," the Pegu Club is a sleek and polished venue, but one that's surprisingly friendly. *77 W. Houston St., 2nd floor (at W. Broadway). www.peguclub.com. ☎ 212/ 473-PEGU (473-7348). Subway: 6/F/M to Bleecker St./Lafayette St.*

Pegu Club

★★ Pianos LOWER EAST SIDE
This multilevel former piano store
gets high marks both as a bar and
as a music venue. On any given
night, three or four different
performances may be going on.
158 Ludlow St. www.pianosnyc.com.
☎ *212/505-3733. Subway: F/M to
Second Ave.*

★★ Rose Bar GRAMERCY PARK
Ian Schrager's head-to-toe renovation of the old Gramercy Park Hotel
included the imaginative redesign of
the bar by artist Julian Schnabel; it's
like the great room in the country
estate of some slightly nutty 21st-
century Venetian prince. *2 Lexington
Ave. (at Gramercy Park N.). www.
gramercyparkhotel.com.* ☎ *212/920-
3300. Subway: 6 to 23rd St.*

★★ The Rum House TIMES
SQUARE   You don't expect to find
a place that's both this hip and this
unpretentious in the heart of Times
Square, but here it is. Set in the
Edison Hotel, this classic watering
hole serves up a mean cocktail and
decent bar food. On some nights, a
live pianist adds to the ambience,
softly playing hits from the days of
Gershwin and Irving Berlin. *228 W.
47th St. (btw. Broadway and Eighth
Ave.). www.edisonrumhouse.com.*
☎ *646/490-6924. Subway: N/Q/R to
49th St.*

*Pianos, a hip music bar set in a former
piano store.*

Russian Samovar MIDTOWN
WEST   With more than 20 house-
made infused vodkas to sample,
this Theater District legend could
make it difficult to get to the theater. The kitschy Russian interpretations of pop standards played on a
white baby grand add to the dizzy-
ing effect of the vodkas. *256 W.
52nd St. (btw. Broadway and Eighth
Ave). www.russiansamovar.com.*
☎ *212/757-0168. Subway: C/E to
50th St.*

Walker's TRIBECA   Before
TriBeCa commanded some of the
top real-estate bucks per square
foot, Walker's was there to serve a
working man a cold brew and a

A classic cocktail at Walker's bar and restaurant.

burger. It's still there and still retains its charm, with cozy tables, a tin ceiling, and a long, conversation-inviting bar. *16 N. Moore St. (at Varick St.). www.walkersnyc.com.* ☎ *212/941-0142. Subway: 1 to Franklin St.*

★★ The West 79th Street Boat Basin Café UPPER WEST SIDE
When spring finally arrives, nature-starved New Yorkers flock here to sip beer on the outdoor patio, mingle under limestone arches, and gaze out at the Hudson River. This is as much a casual restaurant as it is a bar, with hamburgers, hot dogs, and "garden burgers" sizzling on an outdoor grill. *79th Street Boat Basin, 79th St. and the Hudson River. www.boat basincafe.com.* ☎ *212/496-5542. Open Apr-Oct. Subway: 1 to 79th St.*

Dance Clubs

★ **Cielo** MEATPACKING DISTRICT This ultracool space offers top DJs, a state-of-the-art sound system, and an electric ambience sans the snooty attitude (and dumbed-down crowds). *18 Little W. 12th St. (btw. Ninth Ave. and Washington St.). www.cieloclub.com.* ☎ *212/645-5700. $10–$20 cover. Subway: A/C/E to 14th St.*

★★ **Swing 46** MIDTOWN WEST Gotham's active swing dance community supports this wonderful supper club (though you can come to dance without eating). With live music six nights a week (on Mondays a DJ takes over), locals Lindy Hop, jitterbug, waltz, and freestyle well into the wee hours. *349 W. 46th St. (btw. Eighth and Ninth aves.). www.swing46.com.* ☎ *212/ 262-9554. Subway: C or E to 50th St.*

The Gay & Lesbian Scene

★★ **Flaming Saddles** HELLS KITCHEN Yee-haw! This country-western bar is Coyote Ugly reversed, with hot, shirtless male bartenders dancing atop the bar. Along with hunky guys, this place attracts a lot of bachelorette parties, but there's one rule: no "woo-hooing" female customers! *739 Ninth Ave. (at 39th St.).* ☎ *212/713-0481. Subway: C, E to 50th St.*

★ **Henrietta Hudson** WEST VILLAGE This popular ladies' lounge has been calling out to lipstick lesbians since 1991. The theme nights pack the house. *438 Hudson St. (at Morton St.). www. henriettahudson.com.* ☎ *212/924-3347. Subway: 1 to Houston St.*

★★ **Marie's Crisis** WEST VILLAGE The "Church of Show Tunes" is in joyous session 7 nights a week at Marie's Crisis, a basement piano bar that has an atmosphere like no other. In a low-ceilinged room, covered with Christmas lights, dozens of men (and some women) gather each evening to belt out Sondheim, Porter, and Rodgers and Hammerstein. *59 Grove St. (at Seventh Ave.).* ☎ *212/243-9323. Subway: 1 to Christopher St.* ●

Arts & Entertainment **Best Bets**

Most **Unusual Venue**
Bargemusic, *Fulton Ferry Landing, Brooklyn (p 143)*

Best **Free Concerts**
New York Philharmonic Concerts in the Park, *City Parks (p 143)*

Best **World Music**
S.O.B.'s, *204 Varick St. (p 149)*

Best **Historic Venue**
Apollo Theater, *253 W. 125th St. (p 62)*

Best **Food at a Club**
Jazz Standard, *116 E. 27th St. (p 148)*

Best **Classical Dance Troupe**
New York City Ballet, *Lincoln Center, Broadway and 64th St. (p 145)*

Best **Modern Dance Venue**
Joyce Theater, *175 Eighth Ave. (p 145)*

Best **Author Readings**
92nd Street Y, *1395 Lexington Ave. (p 145)*

Best **Off-Broadway Theater**
The Public Theater, *425 Lafayette St. (p 150)*

Best **Comedy Club**
Upright Citizens Brigade, *307 W. 26th St. (p 144)*

Best **Rock-'n'-Roll Bar**
Mercury Lounge, *217 E. Houston St. (p 148)*

Most **Unforgettable Visual Spectacle**
Metropolitan Opera, *Lincoln Center, Broadway and 64th St. (p 150)*

Best **Jazz Club**
Smoke, *2751 Broadway (p 148)*

Most **Cutting-Edge Major Venue**
Brooklyn Academy of Music, *30 Lafayette Ave., Brooklyn (p 75)*

Best **Church Concert Series**
Church of the Transfiguration, *1 E. 29th St. (p 144)*

Previous page: Musical number from the Broadway show On the Town.

Downtown A&E

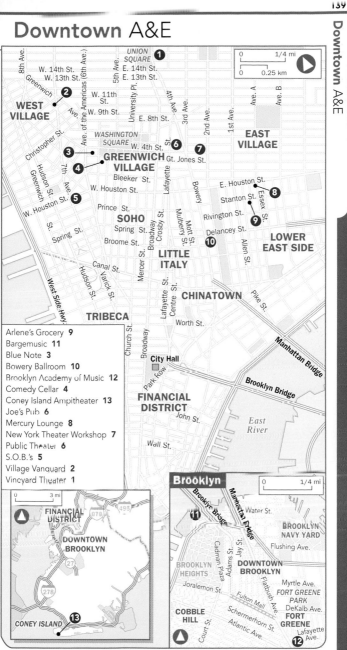

0   1/4 mi
0   0.25 km

8th Ave.
W. 14th St.
W. 13th St.
Greenwich
Ave. of the Americas (6th Ave.)
5th Ave.
E. 14th St.
E. 13th St.
UNION SQUARE ❶

WEST VILLAGE ❷
W. 11th St.
W. 9th St.
University Pl.
4th Ave.
3rd Ave.
2nd Ave.
1st Ave.
Ave. A
Ave. B
E. 8th St.

Christopher St.
WASHINGTON SQUARE
W. 4th St. ❻ ❼
GREENWICH VILLAGE
Gt. Jones St.

EAST VILLAGE

Hudson St.
Greenwich St.
7th Ave.
❸
❹
Bleeker St.
W. Houston St.
Lafayette
Bowery

E. Houston St. ❽
Stanton St.
Essex St.
❾
Rivington St.
Delancey St.
❿

W. Houston St. ❺
Prince St.
Spring St.
Broome St.
SOHO
Broadway
Crosby St.
Mott St.
Mulberry St.
Allen St.

LOWER EAST SIDE

Spring St.
Canal St.
Hudson St.
Varick St.
West Side Hwy.
Mercer St.
LITTLE ITALY
Lafayette St.
Centre St.
CHINATOWN
Pike St.

TRIBECA
Church St.
Broadway
Worth St.

Manhattan Bridge

City Hall
Park Row
Brooklyn Bridge

FINANCIAL DISTRICT
John St.
East River

Wall St.

Arlene's Grocery 9
Bargemusic 11
Blue Note 3
Bowery Ballroom 10
Brooklyn Academy of Music 12
Comedy Cellar 4
Coney Island Ampitheater 13
Joe's Pub 6
Mercury Lounge 8
New York Theater Workshop 7
Public Theater 6
S.O.B.'s 5
Village Vanguard 2
Vineyard Theater 1

0   3 mi
FINANCIAL DISTRICT
495
DOWNTOWN BROOKLYN
27
278
CONEY ISLAND ⓭

Brooklyn
0   1/4 mi

Brooklyn Bridge
Manhattan Bridge
Water St.
⓫
BROOKLYN NAVY YARD
Flushing Ave.
Cadman St.
Adams St.
Jay St.
BROOKLYN HEIGHTS
Joralemon St.
DOWNTOWN BROOKLYN
Myrtle Ave.
FORT GREENE PARK
DeKalb Ave.
Plaza
Fulton Mall
Flatbush Ave.
Schermerhorn Ave.
FORT GREENE
COBBLE HILL
Court St.
Atlantic Ave.
Lafayette Ave.
⓬

Midtown & Uptown A&E

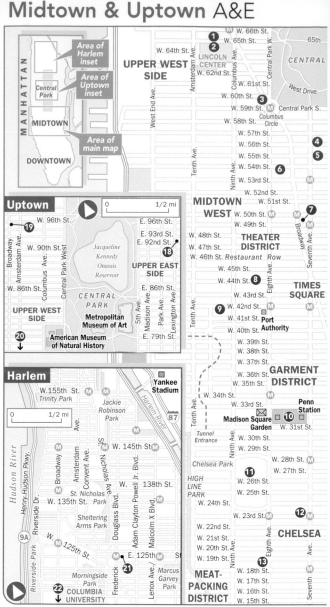

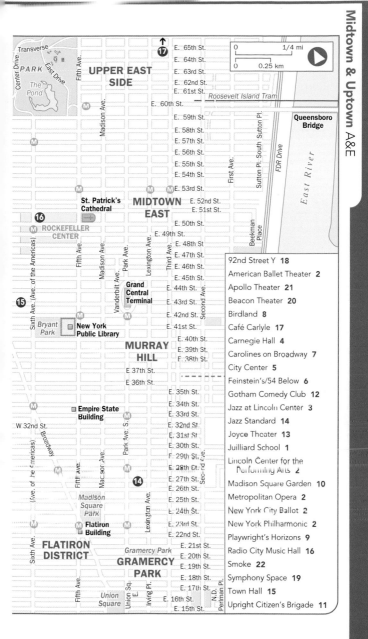

92nd Street Y **18**

American Ballet Theater **2**

Apollo Theater **21**

Beacon Theater **20**

Birdland **8**

Café Carlyle **17**

Carnegie Hall **4**

Carolines on Broadway **7**

City Center **5**

Feinstein's/54 Below **6**

Gotham Comedy Club **12**

Jazz at Lincoln Center **3**

Jazz Standard **14**

Joyce Theater **13**

Juilliard School **1**

Lincoln Center for the Performing Arts **2**

Madison Square Garden **10**

Metropolitan Opera **2**

New York City Ballet **2**

New York Philharmonic **2**

Playwright's Horizons **9**

Radio City Music Hall **16**

Smoke **22**

Symphony Space **19**

Town Hall **15**

Upright Citizen's Brigade **11**

Broadway Theaters

| 0 | 50 y |
| 0 | 50 m |

W. 56th St.
1

W. 55th St.

W. 54th St.
2
NYCVB
Visitor
Information
Center

MIDTOWN
WEST

W. 53rd St.
3
W. 52nd St.
4
5
W. 51st St.
6
7
W. 50th St.
8

W. 49th St.
9
W. 48th St.
10
11
Times Square
Visitors Center
& Broadway
Ticket Center
18

W. 47th St.
12
13 14
TKTS
Booth
17
W. 46th St.   Restaurant Row
15
16
Duffy
Square

W. 45th St.
22
23 24
21
20
30
29 28 27 26
25
Shubert
Alley
W. 44th St.
31 32 33
19
34 35
TIMES
SQUARE

W. 43rd St.
W. 42nd St.
36 37 38
39
W. 41st St.
40
W. 40th St.

W. 39th St.

Ninth Ave.   Eighth Ave.   Broadway   Seventh Ave.   Sixth Ave.   (Avenue of the Americas)

(i) Information
M Subway stop

Al Hirschfeld **30**	Foxwoods **37**	Neil Simon **5**
Ambassador **9**	Gerald Schoenfeld **27**	New Amsterdam **39**
American Airlines **36**	Gershwin **6**	New Victory **38**
August Wilson **4**	Helen Hayes **35**	Palace **17**
Belasco **19**	Imperial **23**	Plymouth **27**
Bernard B. Jacobs **28**	John Golden **29**	Richard Rogers **22**
Booth **26**	Longacre **12**	Samuel J. Friedman **13**
Broadhurst **32**	Lunt-Fontanne **16**	St. James **34**
Broadway **3**	Lyceum **20**	Shubert **33**
Brooks Atkinson **15**	Majestic **31**	Studio 54 **2**
Circle in the Square **7**	Marquis **21**	Vivian Beaumont **1**
Cort **18**	Minskoff **25**	Walter Kerr **11**
Ethel Barrymore **14**	Music Box **24**	Winter Garden **8**
Eugene O'Neill **10**	Nederlander **40**	

A&E Λ lu Z

A chamber ensemble performs at Bargemusic.

Classical Music

★ Bargemusic BROOKLYN
Manhattan skyline views and ethereal tunes as you gently bob on the water—what could be lovelier? An evening at the intimate theater on this permanently docked steel barge, at the foot of the Brooklyn Bridge, is an ideal night out for chamber music lovers. *At Fulton Ferry Landing (just south of the Brooklyn Bridge), Brooklyn. www.bargemusic.org.* ☎ *718/624-2083. Tickets $35, $30 seniors, $15 students. Subway: 2/3 to Clark St.; A/C to High St.*

★★★ Juilliard School LINCOLN CENTER America's premier music school sponsors more than 500 concerts a year, most at no charge, performed by the most talented young people in the nation. *60 Lincoln Center Plaza (Broadway at 65th St.). www.juilliard.edu.* ☎ *212/799-5000. Subway: 1 to 66th St.*

★★★ New York Philharmonic
LINCOLN CENTER Founded in 1842, this is one of the most gifted orchestras anywhere. Its free summertime **Concerts in the Park** take place at green spaces in all five boroughs, and are magical evenings (as are the performances at

the Phil's home theater in Lincoln Center). *At Avery Fisher Hall, Lincoln Center, Broadway and 65th St. www. nyphil.org.* ☎ *212/875-5656 for audience services, 212/875-5030 for box office information, or 212/721-6500 for tickets. Tickets $29–$133. Subway: 1 to 66th St.*

Comedy Clubs

★★ Carolines on Broadway
THEATER DISTRICT Hot headliners come to this upscale club—Jerry Seinfeld, Joel McHale, and Patton Oswalt have all taken the stage. *1626 Broadway (btw 49th and 50th*

Louis C.K. performing at Carolines.

sts.). www.carolines.com. ☎ 212/ 757-4100. $15–$49 cover. Subway: N/R to 49th St.; 1 to 50th St.

★ **Comedy Cellar** GREENWICH VILLAGE   This intimate subterranean club is a favorite among comedy cognoscenti. It gets names you'd expect (Dave Chappelle, Chris Rock) and a few you wouldn't (William Shatner). *117 Macdougal St. (btw. Minetta Lane and W. 3rd St.). www.comedycellar.com.* ☎ *212/254-3480. $10–$24 cover. Subway: A/B/ C/D/E/F/M/S to W. 4th St.*

★ **Gotham Comedy Club** FLATIRON DISTRICT   Big names are frequently on the marquee in this large, 1920s-era space next door to the Chelsea Hotel. The "New Talent Showcase" is a staple. *208 W. 23rd St. (btw. Seventh and Eighth aves.). www.gothamcomedyclub.com.* ☎ *212/367-9000. $12–$30 cover. Subway: F/N/R to 23rd St.*

★★★ **Upright Citizens Brigade** CHELSEA   THE place for improv. Alumni of UCB include Tina Fey, Seth Myers, and Amy Poehler (sometimes they even come back to perform). The company is so popular it now has a second venue at 153 East 3rd Street (though the original theater gets the more

accomplished performers). *307 W. 26th St. (btw. Eighth and Ninth aves.). www.ucbtheatre.com.* ☎ *212/ 366-9176. Subway: 1 to 23rd St.*

Dance

★★★ **American Ballet Theater** LINCOLN CENTER   ABT is renowned for its dazzling story ballets—*Coppelia, Swan Lake, Sleeping Beauty*—and tends to produce more bravura stars than the New York City Ballet (below), which focuses more on ensemble works. *Metropolitan Opera House, Lincoln Center, Broadway and 64th. www.abt.org.* ☎ *212/477-3030. Subway: 1 to 66th St.*

★★ **City Center** MIDTOWN WEST   Alvin Ailey, Bill T. Jones/ Arnie Zanes, and Paul Taylor perform here, along with other major dance companies. You'll understand why, once you've attended a show in this splendid, Moorish-revival space (formerly a temple). In the basement are the stages of the excellent off-Broadway Manhattan Theatre Club. *131 W. 55th St. (btw. Sixth and Seventh aves.). www.city center.org.* ☎ *877/247-0430. Tickets $10–$150. Subway: F/N/Q/R/W to 57th St.; B/D/E to Seventh Ave.*

Heavenly Sounds

New York churches may play traditional hymns during their religious services, but many also host afternoon and evening concerts in a variety of secular styles, from classical to opera, from instrumental to thrilling soloists. And the price is right: A few concerts require tickets, but most have a "requested donation" from $2 to $10. Check the websites for schedules. Some of the best include **Church of the Transfiguration** (1 E. 29th St.; www.little church.org), **St. Bart's** (325 Park Ave.; www.stbarts.org), **St. Paul's Chapel and Trinity Church** (p 16), **the Cathedral of St. John the Divine** (p 61), and **St. Ignatius Loyola** (980 Park Ave.; www.stigna tiusloyola.org).

New York City Ballet dancers perform at Lincoln Center.

★★ Joyce Theater CHELSEA

In this renovated Art Deco–era movie theater, the audience sits slightly above the dancers, meaning that you won't be seeing just the feet or just the bodies—you'll get the whole picture. In past years, Pilobolus has performed here, as well as the Twyla Tharp Company, Wendy Whelan, and BodyTraffic. *175 Eighth Ave. (at 19th St.). www.joyce.org.* ☎ *212/691-9740. Tickets $36–$71. Subway: C/E to 23rd St.; 1 to 18th St.*

★★★ New York City Ballet

LINCOLN CENTER   The legendary George Balanchine founded this stellar company, which still performs his diamond-sharp choreography. *At the New York State Theater, Lincoln Center, Broadway and 64th St. www.nycballet.com* 📱 *212/870-5570. Tickets $30–$179. Subway: 1 to 66th St.*

Landmark Venues

★★ 92nd Street Y UPPER EAST

SIDE   Forget what you know about the YMCA—this Jewish community center offers concerts, literary readings, and superb cultural events with the top newsmakers of the day. *1395 Lexington Ave. (at 92nd St.). www.92y.org.* ☎ *212/415-5500. Ticket prices vary. Subway: 4/5/6 to 86th St.; 6 to 96th St.*

★★ Apollo Theater HARLEM

A legendary institution, with annual jazz concerts and a popular Amateur Night on Wednesdays. *See p 62.*

★★★ Brooklyn Academy of Music BROOKLYN

Just 25 minutes by subway from Midtown, the five theaters that make up this renowned arts institution bring in the most cutting-edge performances of theater, opera, dance, and music (Peter Brooks, Philip Glass, and more) from around the world. *30 Lafayette Ave. (off Flatbush Ave.), and 651 Fulton St., Brooklyn. www.bam.org.* ☎ *718/636-4100. Ticket prices vary. Subway: 2/3/4/5/B/D/M/N/Q/R to Atlantic Ave./Barclays Center.*

★★★ Carnegie Hall MIDTOWN

WEST   Perhaps the world's most famous performance space, Carnegie Hall boasts everything from world-renowned orchestras to solo sitar stars in its three concert halls (big, medium and small). Tickets for the 1-hour tours (offered Oct–late June) are available at the box office. ⏱ *1 hr. (for tour). 881 Seventh Ave. (at 56th St.). www.carnegiehall.org.* ☎ *212/247-7800. Ticket prices vary. Tours $17 adults, $12 students and seniors. Tours Mon–Fri 11:30am, 12:30, 2, and 3pm; Sat 11:30am and 12:30pm; Sun 12:30pm. Subway: A/B/C/D/1 to Columbus Circle; N/Q/R/W to 57th St./Seventh Ave.*

★★★ Lincoln Center for the Performing Arts UPPER WEST

SIDE   One of the most important cultural complexes on the planet. See individual listings for the **American Ballet Theater** (p 144), **Jazz at Lincoln Center** (p 148), **Juilliard School** (p 143), **New York Philharmonic** (p 143), **New York City Ballet** (p 145), and **Metropolitan Opera** (p 150) for more information. *10 Lincoln Center Plaza*

Radio City Music Hall.

(Broadway from 62nd–66th sts.).
www.lincolncenter.org. ☎ 212/875-5456. Ticket prices vary. Subway: 1 to 66th St.

★★★ Radio City Music Hall
MIDTOWN WEST This stunning 6,200-seat Art Deco theater is home to the annual Christmas Spectacular and the Rockettes, plus many concerts throughout the year. See p 9.

★ Symphony Space UPPER
WEST SIDE Now in its 35th year, this innovative institution offers a varied program of dance, film, readings, and music. We particularly like the "New Voices" series of concerts from young Broadway composers. 2537 Broadway (at 95th St.). www.symphonyspace.org. ☎ 212/864-5400. Tickets $25–$40. Subway: 1/2/3 to 96th St.

★ Town Hall MIDTOWN WEST
A National Historic Site, Town Hall has pin-drop acoustics and has hosted performers ranging from Elvis Costello to Pink Martini, the Klezmatics and flamenco singers. 123 W. 43rd St. (btw. Sixth and Seventh aves.). www.thetownhall.org.

☎ 212/840-2824. Tickets $24–$150. Subway: N/Q/R/S/W/1/2/3/7 to 42nd St./Times Sq.; B/D/F/M to 42nd St.

Live Music
Arlene's Grocery LOWER EAST SIDE A casual rock club with a good sound system; great bang for the buck. 95 Stanton St. (btw. Ludlow and Orchard sts.). www.arlenesgrocery.net. ☎ 212/358-1633. $8–$10 cover; no cover Mon. Subway: F to Second Ave.

★★★ Beacon Theater UPPER
WEST SIDE Every seat at this Art Deco landmark has a good view, and while you won't get the meganames, you will see talented stars either on the way up or down, such as Tedeschi Trucks Band, Cyndi Lauper, and comedian Jerry Seinfeld. 2124 Broadway (at 74th St.). www.beacontheatre.com. ☎ 212/465-6500. Subway: 1/2/3 to 72nd St.

★★ Birdland MIDTOWN WEST
This legendary jazz club is one of the few (beyond Jazz at Lincoln Center) with room for really big bands. The weekly **Jim Caruso's Cast Party,** an open mic night for

Marquee above the Ambassador Theater, in the Broadway Theater District.

Choosing the Right Broadway Show

You can traipse the entire Metropolitan Museum of Art, attend a Yankees game, and ascend to the top of the Empire State Building, but you can't really say you've done New York until you spend an evening at the theater. It's an essential element in a NYC vacation. Once you've accepted that you may not be able to score tickets to a mega-hit like *Hamilton*, how do you choose from among the many other shows? *Some tips:* Avoid shows that have been running for over two years, as they won't have the electricity of a younger show (the casts get bored). And look at whether the show garnered Tony nominations; that's a good measure for how high quality the production is (this info can be easily googled and compared). Finally, don't forget that Off-Broadway shows can be as satisfying (and often as filled with stars). To save money on a show see "Getting Broadway Tickets" (p 149); for where the Broadway theaters are, see our map on p 142.

Broadway performers (and would-be ones), is a hoot. *315 W. 44th St. (btw. Eighth and Ninth aves.). www. birdlandjazz.com.* ☎ *212/581-3080. Tickets $10–$40. Subway: A/C/E to 42nd St.*

Blue Note GREENWICH VILLAGE The Blue Note has the most corporate feel of the city's jazz clubs (it's now a multinational chain). Tables are jammed together, the bar area is even more crowded, and the second floor is given over to a huge souvenir stand. But since it still attracts genuine talent, it can't be overlooked. *131 W. 3rd St. (at Sixth Ave.). www.bluenote.net.* ☎ *212/475-8592. Tickets $20–$55. Subway: A/B/C/D/E/F/M to W. 4th St.*

★★ **Bowery Ballroom** LOWER EAST SIDE Another Art Deco wonder– this one with a big stage and good sightlines from every

Birdland jazz.

corner. Such alt-rockers as Kurt Vile perform here, as do stalwarts like Emmylou Harris. *6 Delancey St. (at Bowery). www.boweryballroom.com.* ☎ *212/533-2111. Tickets $13–$40. Subway: F/J/M/Z to Delancey St.*

★ **Café Carlyle** UPPER EAST SIDE This classic cabaret lounge is the venue of choice for a rotating lineup of musical stars; Woody Allen and his New Orleans–style jazz band perform often. *Carlyle Hotel, 35 E. 76th St. www.thecarlyle. com.* ☎ *212/744-1600. Tickets $55–$170. Subway: 6 to 77th St.*

★★ **Coney Island Amphitheater** BROOKLYN An outdoor, but covered venue, this became *the* place to go for summer pop music when it opened in 2016. Concert-goers stroll the iconic boardwalk, and ride the rides, in the afternoon, before heading in to listen to the likes of Eryka Badu or Boston. *3052 W. 21st (at the Boardwalk in Coney Island; www.coneyislandlive.com. Prices vary. Subway: D,F,N,Q to Coney Island/Stillwell Ave.*

★★ **Feinstein's/54 Below** MIDTOWN WEST Another cabaret venue but with a twist: The majority of the entertainers who perform here are playing hooky from their real jobs at the big Broadway houses nearby—like Patty Lupone and Matthew Morrison (of *Glee*). The club itself is charming, with a 1930s speakeasy decor. *254 W. 54th St. (btw. Eighth Ave. and Broadway). www.54below.com.* ☎ *646/476-3551. Prices vary. Subway: C/E to 50th St.*

★★★ **Jazz at Lincoln Center** UPPER WEST SIDE The gold standard, meaning that the biggest stars in the genre vie to play in these three spectacular venues (two with eye-popping views of Central Park behind the musicians). Director of the program, legendary trumpeter Wynton Marsalis, helms the in-house orchestra. *In the Time Warner Center (at Broadway and 60th St.). www.jalc. org.* ☎ *212/258-9800. Prices vary. Subway 1/A/E/C to 59th St.*

★★ **Jazz Standard** MURRAY HILL One of the city's largest jazz clubs, Jazz Standard has a retro vibe and the best food of any club. (It's part of, and downstairs from, **Blue Smoke,** a renowned barbecue joint.) *116 E. 27th St. (btw. Park Ave. S. and Lexington Ave.). www.jazz standard.net.* ☎ *212/576-2232. $25–$35 cover. Subway: 6 to 28th St.*

★★★ **Joe's Pub** EAST VILLAGE Located in the Public Theater and named for its founder, Joseph Papp, this eclectic supper club hosts a range of performers from monologists to world music to hip hop, often by emerging stars (and some big names, too). *425 Lafayette St. (btw. Astor Place and E. 4th St.). www.joespub.com.* ☎ *212/539-8778. Subway: 6 to Astor Place.*

Madison Square Garden GARMENT DISTRICT Billy Joel has a "residency" here; he's just one of the mega-names in popular music that regularly play this cavernous 20,000-seat arena. *Seventh Ave. (from 31st–33rd sts.). www.the garden.com.* ☎ *212/465-MSG1 (465-6741). Ticket prices vary. Subway: A/C/E/1/2/3 to 34th St.*

★★ **Mercury Lounge** LOWER EAST SIDE The ideal live-music rock-'n'-roll bar. Top talent, just the right amount of grit. *217 E. Houston St. (btw. Essex and Ludlow sts.). www.mercuryloungenyc.com.* ☎ *212/260-4700. $10–$12 cover; some shows require tickets. Subway: F to Second Ave.*

★★ **Smoke** UPPER WEST SIDE Going strong for almost 14 years—and even despite expanding and adding a supper club—Smoke still hasn't forgotten its initial objective

Smoke Jazz & Supper Club.

gigs, 2751 Broadway (btw. 105th and 106th sts.). www.smokejazz.com. ☎ 212/864-6662. $35 cover Fri–Sat. Subway: 1 to 103rd St.

★ **S.O.B.'s** SOHO   This top world-music venue features Brazilian, Caribbean, and Latin beats. The music is so hot, you won't be able to stay in your seat. *204 Varick St. (at W. Houston St.). www.sobs. com.* ☎ *212/243-4940. $10–$32 cover. Subway: 1 to Houston St.*

★★★ **The Village Vanguard** GREENWICH VILLAGE   Since 1935, this club has been showcasing jazz artists. Many of the greats, including Sonny Rollins and John Coltrane, have recorded live jazz albums here. *178 Seventh Ave. S. (just below 11th St.). www.villagevanguard.com.* ☎ *212/255-4037. Tickets $20–$25; 1-drink minimum. Subway: 1/2/3 to 14th St.*

of offering intimate, reliable jazz. Such mainstays as Mike LeDonne, John Farnsworth, and Eric Alexander, who helped launch Smoke, still make it their home with regular

Getting Broadway Tickets

On average, only five or six shows per year get away with charging full price for their seats eight shows per week. For those productions, buying advance tickets well in advance from **TeleCharge** (www.telecharge.com; ☎ 212/239-6200) or **Ticketmaster** (www.ticketmaster. com; ☎ 212/307-4100) is key. With other shows you have the option of buying in advance or day of, and getting discounts of up to 50% through such websites as www.broadwaybox.com and www. playbill.com. The app **TodayTix** (for day- and week-of shows) is also a primo discount getter. I think using these websites is preferable to waiting on line at the **TKTS booth** (www.tdf.org; ☎ 212/912-9770), since that eats up your valuable vacation time. Still, good show discounts can be had at the **Times Square booth** (47th St. and Broadway; Mon and Wed–Sat 3–8pm, Tues 2–7pm, and, for matinees only, Wed and Sat 10am–2pm, and Sun 11am–2pm); the **South Street Seaport TKTS booth** (Mon–Sat 11am–6pm, Sun 11am–4pm; corner of Front and John sts), and in **Downtown Brooklyn** (1 MetroTech Center, at Jay St. and Myrtle Ave.; Tues–Sat 11am–6pm). Most tickets are sold at half-price, although some are discounted only 25%. A $4 TKTS service charge is added. *Tip:* Keep the ticket stubs if you plan to use TKTS more than once in a week; they'll allow you to jump the line the second time.

Opera-goers head for the Metropolitan Opera House on Lincoln Center Plaza.

Off-Broadway Theaters

★★ New York Theater Workshop

EAST VILLAGE   Intellectually heady and sometimes avant-garde, this company has launched some big hits, such as *Once* (Tony Award) and *Rent* (Pulitzer Prize). *79 E. 4th St., (btw. Second Ave. and the Bowery). www.nytw.org. ☎ 212/460-5475; subway: 6 to Astor Place.*

★ Playwrights Horizons

MIDTOWN WEST   Dedicated to nurturing the art of the writer (lyricists and librettists as well as playwrights), Playwrights has always had a great eye for talent, producing the works of Stephen Sondheim, Christopher Durang and A. R. Gurney. *416 W. 42nd St. (btw. Seventh and Eighth aves). www.playwrightshorizons.org. ☎ 212/564-1235. Subway: 1/2/3/N/Q/R/ S to Times Sq. or A/E/C to 42nd St.*

★★★ Public Theater

NOHO Come here for groundbreaking stagings of Shakespeare's plays as well as new plays, musicals (*Hamilton* started here!), classical dramas, and solo performances. *425 Lafayette St. (btw. Astor Place and E. 4th St.). www.publictheater.org. ☎ 212/539-8500. Ticket prices vary. Subway: 6 to Astor Place.*

The Vineyard Theater

UNION SQUARE   The biggest risk-taker of the major Off-Broadway theaters, the Vineyard Theater presents out-and-out performance art along with less far-out plays and musicals. When they're good, they're great; even when their shows miss the mark, they're still usually intriguing. *Avenue Q* (Tony Award) debuted here before moving to Broadway. *108 E. 15th St., off Union Sq. www.vineyardtheatre.org. ☎ 212/353-0303. Subway: 4/5 6/ N/Q/R/L to Union Sq.*

Opera

★★★ Metropolitan Opera

LINCOLN CENTER   Opera aficionados consider this one of the most electrifying companies in the world. *At the Metropolitan Opera House, Lincoln Center, Broadway and 64th St. www.metoperafamily.org. ☎ 212/362-6000. Tickets $17–$295. Subway: 1 to 66th St.*

New York City Opera

AROUND TOWN   Though it has risen from the ashes, NYC Opera is a shadow of its former self, offering only a handful of performances each year. *At differ venues across the city. www.nycopera.com. Ticket prices vary.*

Hotel Best Bets

Most Romantic
Inn at Irving Place $$$ *56 Irving Place (p 159)*

Hotel with the Best Restaurant & Bar
The NoMad $$$ *1170 Broadway (p 162)*

Best Boutique Hotel
Crosby Street Hotel $$$
79 Crosby St. (p 158)

Best Old-School Glamour
The Beekman $$$$ *123 Nassau St. (p 156)*

Most Luxurious Hotel
The Peninsula—New York $$$$
700 Fifth Ave. (p 162)

Best Budget Hotel
Nesva Hotel $ *39–12 29th St. (at 39th Ave.), Long Island City, Queens (p 161)*

Best for Kids
Hotel Beacon $$$$ *230 Broadway (p 159)*

Best Value
NobleDen $$–$$$ *196 Grand St. (p 162)*

Best Service
The Surrey $$$$ *20 E. 76th St. (p 164)*

Best Hotel in the Middle of Everything
The Knickerbocker $$$
151 W. 54th St. (p 160)

Best for Celebrity Sightings
Gramercy Park Hotel $$$$
2 Lexington Ave. (p 158)

Best Hotel Pool
The Greenwich Hotel $$$
377 Greenwich St. (p 159)

Best for Business Travelers
The Beekman $$ *123 Nassau St. (p 156);* and The Benjamin $$$ *125 E. 50th St. (p 157)*

Previous page: The mod-chic lobby of the Crosby Street Hotel.

Downtown Hotels

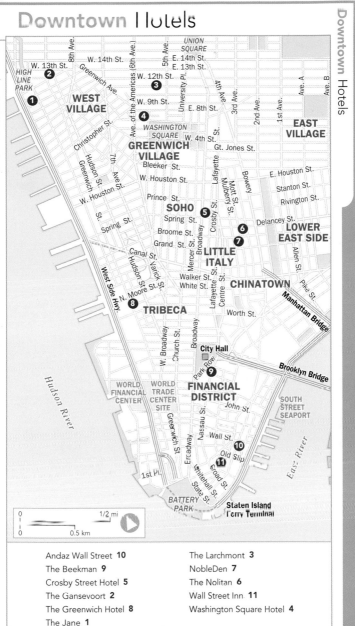

Midtown & Uptown Hotels

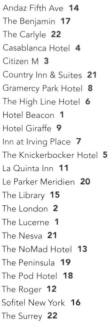

Hotels A to Z

Room 214 at the Ace Hotel.

★★ **Ace Hotel** FLATIRON DISTRICT   Ultrahip but attitude-free, this Pacific Coast transplant has some of the coolest amenities in town: Gibson guitars and turntables in rooms! Pendelton wool blankets on beds! Mini-Heineken kegs in full-size fridges! On top of that, there's a room for every budget (the cheapest option is bunk beds). Has a warm, buzzing lobby and a hot restaurant (**the Breslin;** p 118). *20 W. 29th St. (btw. Fifth Ave. and Broadway). www.acehotel.com/new york.* ☎ *212/678-2222. 273 units. Double $139–$539. AE, DISC, MC, V. Subway: N/R to 28th St.*

★★ **Andaz Fifth Avenue** MIDTOWN   Behind a nameless facade lies one of the city's smartest hotels. The striking interior of this historic 1916 building has become a thoughtful homage to the city, with tall, factory-style shutters and edgy artwork. Rooms have extravagantly high ceilings, rainfall shower heads, and soaking tubs. Some have spectacular views of the New York Public Library, across the street. *485 Fifth Ave. (at 41st St.). www.newyork.5thavenue.andaz.hyatt. com.* ☎ *212/601-1233. 184 units. Double from $247, suite from $429. AE, DISC, MC, V. Subway: 4/5/6 to Grand Central and B/D/F to Bryant Park/42nd St.*

★ **Andaz Wall Street** WALL STREET   The dazzling lobby, bar, and restaurant were designed by David Rockwell; the minimalist rooms, alas, lack the sparkle of the public spaces. But the high ceilings and oak floors give the rooms a solid, grounded feel. Plus, you gotta love the complimentary Wi-Fi and minibar (sans alcohol). *75 Wall St. (at Water St.). www.newyork.wall street.andaz.hyatt.com.* ☎ *212/590-1234. 253 units. Double $195–$495. AE, DISC, MC, V. Subway: 2/3 to Wall St./William St. or 4/5 to Wall St.*

★★★ **The Beekman** FINANCIAL DISTRICT   Opened in 2016, this dazzler restores one of the city's first skyscrapers, built in 1901. Over the mink bar is a soaring 9-story atrium, with a pyramidal glass skylight; next to it is a restaurant by celeb chef Tom Colicchio (he's also in charge of room service). Rooms are carved out of former offices, so each has a different shape and size, but all share quietly elegant furnishings. **Tip:** ask for a room overlooking Nassau Street, so you don't get noise from the construction project next door (expected to last through 2018). *123 Nassau St. (at Beekman St.). www.thompsonhotels. com. ☎ 212/233-2300. 287 rooms. Doubles from $299, suites from $459. AE, DISC, MC, V. Subway: 4/5/6/R Brooklyn Bridge/City Hall, 2/3 Park Pl., A/C Fulton St.*

★★ **The Benjamin** MIDTOWN EAST   Set in a 1927 landmark building, the Benjamin combines solid bones with top-flight service and amenities. You will be supremely comfortable here. *125 E. 50th St. (at Lexington Ave.). www. thebenjamin.com. ☎ 212/715-2500. 209 units. Double from $161, suite from $399. AE, DC, DISC, MC, V. Subway: 6 to 51st St.; E/F to Lexington Ave.*

★★★ **The Carlyle** UPPER EAST SIDE   The old-school glamour in this 1930 white-glove landmark is tasteful, understated, never over-the-top. But baby, it's plenty luxe, all gleaming marble and custom fabrics. **Bemelman's Bar** (see p 132) is a jewel. *35 E. 76th St. (at Madison Ave.). www.rosewoodhotels. com/thecarlyle. ☎ 212/744-1600. 188 units. Double $389–$950, suite from $950. AE, DC, DISC, MC, V. Subway: 6 to 51st St.; E/F to Lexington Ave.*

★★ **Casablanca Hotel** TIMES SQUARE   An oasis in the middle of the Times Square mayhem, the Casablanca is one of the best moderate options in the area. Rooms are good-size for the price, and a homey lounge with fireplace where daily complimentary wine and cheese and breakfast are served adds to the value. Book early—the word is out on the Casablanca. *147 W.43rd St. (btw. Broadway and Sixth Ave). www.casablancahotel.com. ☎ 212/869-1212. 48 units. Double $212–$500. AE, DC, MC, V. Subway: N/R/Q/1/2/3 to Times Sq.–42nd St.*

★★ **Citizen M** TIMES SQUARE   On a budget? Try these unapologetically pre-fab, tiny, shiny white

Atrium shot of the Grand Salon at the Beekman Hotel.

A rooftop deck at Times Square's Citizen M hotel.

"pod" rooms, each with a modular shower/toilet enclosed unit, and a huge bed that pushes right up to a wall-to-wall window, with bright red pillows bearing notes encouraging pillow fights. The lobby is a hipster haunt, as is the roof bar. *218 W. 50th St. (btw. Seventh and Eighth Aves). www.citizenm.com.* ☎ *212/461-3638. $141–$338 double. Subway: C/E to 50th St, B/D to Seventh Ave or N/R to 49th St.*

Country Inn & Suites QUEENS Just one and a half blocks from a subway stop that's one stop from Manhattan—that's the main attraction of this Queens cookie-cutter chain motel. Oh, and the prices are excellent. *40–34 Crescent St. (near 41st Ave.), Long Island City, Queens. www.countryinns.com.* ☎ *800/830-5222 or 718/729-2111. 48 units. $80–$124 double. Subway: N/Q to 39th Ave.*

★★ Crosby Street Hotel SOHO Finding a hotel this light and irresistibly playful in the long, dark shadows of Crosby Street is a revelation. Spacious rooms are done in muted hues—mauve, plum, apple—with plumped linens and textured fabrics. It's elegant and whimsical all at once. *79 Crosby St. (btw. Prince and Spring sts.). http://crosbystreethotel.com.* ☎ *212/226-6400. 86 units. Double $595–$715, suite $815–$2,250. AE, DC, MC, V. Subway: N/R to Prince St.; 6 to Spring St.*

★ The Gansevoort MEATPACKING DISTRICT This stylish spot has transcended its annoying initial trendiness and established itself as a reliable choice for service and comfort. It has spacious rooms, a full-service spa, and a rooftop pool. **Plunge,** the rooftop bar, has 360-degree views. *18 Ninth Ave. (at 13th St.). www.hotelgansevoort.com.* ☎ *877/426-7386. 187 units. Double $184–$725, duplex penthouse $5,000. AE, MC, V. Subway: A/C/E to 14th St.*

★★ Gramercy Park Hotel GRAMERCY PARK Built in 1925, this legend was brought back to life a little over a decade ago by owners who added 21st-century technology and a big dollop of elegance. Many of the large rooms have views of charming Gramercy Park, and all feature velvet upholstered beds, leather-topped tables,

The Gansevoort, in the Meatpacking District.

and photos by world famous photojournalists. Public spaces include the fabulous Rose Bar and Danny Meyer's Italian gem of a restaurant, Maialino. *2 Lexington Ave. (at 21st St.). www.gramercyparkhotel.com. ☎ 212/920-3300. 185 units. Double $400–$700. AE, DC, MC, V. Subway: 6 to 23rd St.*

★★★ The Greenwich Hotel

TRIBECA   No detail or expense has been spared at this beautiful small luxury hotel (whose owners include Robert De Niro), where even the bricks are handcrafted. It's meant to feel like an 88-room home—if home is a rustically elegant country manor filled with art and antiques. It's everything a hip, edgy downtown hotel isn't—and that makes it plenty hip. *377 Greenwich St. (at N. Moore St.). www.the greenwichhotel.com. ☎ 212/941-8900. 88 units. Double $585–$725, suite $995–$1,750. AE, DC, DISC, MC, V. Subway: 1 to Franklin St.*

★★★ The High Line Hotel

CHELSEA   Very few NYC hotels deserve the high price tag they wear. This one just may. Set in a former ecclesiastical building (a beaut of a red-brick Victorian), the High Line Hotel looms like a castle over Tenth Avenue. Its interior is as grand, though delightfully quirky, with rooms that look like they could have been inhabited by a Gatsby type in the 1920s. And the hotel has outdoor courtyards and restaurants that are a delight in the warm weather months. *180 Tenth Ave. (at 20th St.). www.thehighlinehotel.com. ☎ 212/929-3888. 60 units. $209–$489 basic double. Subway: C to 23rd St.*

★ Hotel Beacon UPPER WEST

SIDE   This solid, family-friendly choice is a short walk from **Central Park** (p 100) and the **American Museum of Natural History** (p 50). The good-value perks include large rooms with kitchenettes. *230 Broadway (at 75th St.). www.beacon hotel.com. ☎ 800/572-4969. 260 units. Double $209–$349, suite $355 and up. AE, DC, MC, V. Subway: 1/2/3 to 72nd St.*

★★ Hotel Giraffe FLATIRON

DISTRICT   This boutique property never fails to impress. Book early to snag one of the stylish, elegant guest rooms graced with high ceilings, velveteen upholstered chairs, and a soothing slate-gray palette. Deluxe rooms have small balconies. *365 Park Ave. S. (at 26th St.). www. hotelgiraffe.com. ☎ 212/685-7700. 72 units. Double $225–$500 w/ breakfast. AE, DC, MC, V. Subway: 6 to 28th St.*

★★ Inn at Irving Place

GRAMERCY   Bored with sleek minimalism? This 170-year-old town house marries 19th-century elegance with 21st-century luxe (antique beds plumped up with Frette linens). Spacious rooms have antiques and art, nonworking fireplaces, and big bathrooms. *56 Irving Place (btw. 17th and 18th sts.). www.innatirving.com. ☎ 800/685-1447. 12 units. Double $395–$645. AE, DC, MC, V. Subway: N/R/4/5/6 to 14th St./Union Sq.*

The discreet entrance to the High Line Hotel.

THE HIGH LINE HOTEL

A cabin room at The Jane.

★ The Jane WEST VILLAGE

Two-thirds of the units in this "micro hotel" are 50-square-foot spaces complete with bed (or bunk bed), flatscreen TV, Wi-Fi, A/C, and shared bathrooms—all yours for $125 a night. But with such fabulous public spaces—a massive lobby bar with fireplace, a rooftop lounge overlooking the Hudson River—who needs a big, pricey room to rattle around in? *113 Jane St. (at the West Side Hwy.). www.the janenyc.com. ☎ 212/924-6700. 210 units. Room $125–$250. AE, MC, V. Subway: A/C/E to 14th St.*

★★ The Knickerbocker TIMES SQUARE

Set in a landmarked, 1902 Beaux Arts knockout of a skyscraper, this hotel makes smart use of the building's grand bones: Guest rooms all have soaring ceilings and massive windows. Topnotch service, zen decor, and amenities such as on-site gourmet restaurants keep things calm in the midst of all the Times Square hoopla. *6 Times Square (on 42nd St., near Broadway). www.theknickerbocker.com. ☎ 212/204-4980. 230 units. $225—$565 double. Subway: 1/2/3/7/N/R/Q/S to 42nd St./Times Sq.*

★ The Larchmont Hotel GREENWICH VILLAGE

Almost all of the rooms here share bathrooms, keeping the prices reasonable. Other than that inconvenience, this is a fine place to stay: a Beaux-Art era brownstone, it's kept spick-and-span, with simple furnishings but good beds, and one of the best locations in the Village—a charming, tree-lined street, near a number of subway lines. *27 W. 11th St. (btw. Fifth and Sixth aves.). www.larchmont hotel.com. ☎ 212/989-9333. 62 units. $119 single, $129 double, $219 family room with private bathroom. Continental breakfast included in rate. AE, MC, V. Children 12 and under stay free. Subway: A/B/C/D/E/F to W. 4th St.*

★ La Quinta Inn MIDTOWN WEST

The location in the heart of Koreatown (with good Korean BBQs and karaoke bars up and down the street) is 2 blocks from the **Empire State Building** (p 7) and **Macy's** (p 92). The spacious if style-free rooms have amenities you wouldn't expect from a moderate-priced

The lobby of Le Parker Meridien.

hotel, such as free Wi-Fi. Or you can enjoy the fresh air at the rooftop bar instead. *17 W. 32nd St. (btw. Fifth Ave. and Broadway). www. applecorehotels.com or www.lq.com.* ☎ *800/567-7720. 182 units. Double $119–$240. AE, DC, DISC, MC, V. Subway: B/D/F/M/N/R to 34th St.*

★★ **Le Parker Meridien** MID-TOWN WEST   The lobby's soaring atrium puts you squarely in a New York state of mind; it's a bustling spot, with a sexy Moroccan-style lobby bar **(the Knave)** in one corner and a roadhouse burger spot **(Burger Joint**—which makes one of the best burgers in the city, p 118) tucked in another. This 42-floor hotel has guest rooms decorated in olive, orange, and brown hues, and they're spiffy indeed. Cheeky, too: The hotel's "DO NOT DISTURB" signs read "FUHGEDDABOUDIT." The rooftop pool has Central Park views. *119 W. 56th St. (btw. Sixth and Seventh aves.). www.parkermeridien.com.* ☎ *212/245-5000. 725 units. Double $229–$600, suite $780 and up. AE, DC, DISC, MC, V. Subway: B/D/E to Seventh Ave.*

★ **The Library Hotel** MIDTOWN EAST   Each of the 10 floors here is dedicated to a major category of the Dewey Decimal System. Rooms have a Deco elegance, done in buttery yellow and loaded with books to read. The Petite Rooms are a solid value, but yes, quite petite. The **Writer's Den,** on the 14th floor, has the dog-eared feel of a beloved book. *299 Madison Ave. (at 41st St.). www.libraryhotel.com* ☎ *212/983 1500. 60 units, Double $239 $500. AE, DC, MC, V. Subway: 4/5/6/7/S to 42nd St.*

★★ **The London** MIDTOWN WEST   In the heart of Manhattan, the sleek and fashionable London has plenty to offer, including, most importantly, spacious rooms with spectacular city views. Suites

The Lucerne, set in a classic Beaux Arts skyscraper on the Upper West Side.

feature separate parlors, some with French doors. *151 W. 54th St (btw. Sixth and Seventh aves.). www.the londonnyc.com.* ☎ *866/690-2029. 562 units. Double $284–$800. AE, DC, MC, V. Subway: B, D, E to Seventh Ave.*

The Lucerne UPPER WEST SIDE A handy location—close to Central Park, the Museum of Natural History, and all the charm of the Upper West Side—makes this hotel, housed in a classic Beaux Arts skyscraper, a solid moderate choice. The service is friendly, and rooms are well equipped and big enough for kings, queens, or two doubles. Suites have kitchenettes, making it a good choice for families. Some rooms even have views of the Hudson River. *201 W. 79th St. (at Amsterdam Ave.). www.thelucerne hotel.com.* ☎ *212/875-1000. 200 units. Double $166–$250. AE, DC, DISC, MC, V. Subway: 1 to 79th St.*

★ **Nesva Hotel** QUEENS   Very pleasant rooms with quality beds and non-cookie-cutter contemporary decor make staying in nowheresville Queens more than palatable.

Rooftop party space at the NoMad hotel.

Another huge plus is that the hotel's area is safe and just two stops from midtown Manhattan. *39–12 29th St. (at 39th Ave.), Long Island City, Queens. www.nesvahotel.com.* ☎ *917/745-1000. 36 units. $140– $154 double. Subway: N, Q to 39th Ave.*

★★ **NobleDen** CHINATOWN Mostly Europeans book this sleek new hotel, which sits on the porous border between Chinatown and Little Italy. My guess is they're drawn by the clean Scandinavian-style design (lots of neutral colors offset by pops of red, hidden drawers that double your storage space, angular lamps, and two-room bathrooms). I like the king units best for their floor- to- ceiling windows. *196 Grand St. (btw. Mulberry and Mott sts.). www.nobleden.com.* ☎ *212/ 390-8988. 54 units. $198–$284 double. Subway: B, D to Grand St. or N, Q, R, 6 to Canal St.*

★ **The Nolitan** NOLITA Located close to Chinatown, Little Italy, Soho, and Nolita, the Nolitan fits in snugly with those unique neighborhoods. This boutique charmer features cozy rooms, many with balconies, all with open views from oversize windows. The hotel even offers free bike rentals to better explore the downtown neighborhoods. *30 Kenmare St. (btw. Elizabeth and Mott sts.). www.nolitan hotel.com.* ☎ *212/925-2556. 55 units. Double $159–$483. AE, DC, MC, V. Subway: 6 to Spring St.*

★★★ **The NoMad** FLATIRON DISTRICT Circular bedrooms— those are the lure for the honeymooners who go for the suites at this swank hotel. But even the cheaper digs are sensual, with fabric dressing screens dividing the rooms, beds piled high with fluffy duvets, a European *fin de siècle* vibe, and unique art on the walls. Room service comes from the superb **NoMad Restaurant** (see p 34). *1170 Broadway (at 28th St.). www.thenomadhotel.com.* ☎ *212/ 796-1500. 168 units. $295–$575 double. Subway: N, R, 6 to 28th St.*

★★★ **The Peninsula—New York** MIDTOWN A dream of a hotel, almost perfect in every way. Housed in a 1905 landmark building, the Peninsula has some of the most tastefully luxurious (and priciest) rooms in town. Take the curving stairway up from the world-class spa to the 22nd-floor heated pool,

The ultra-luxe Peninsula Hotel.

with Central Park and Fifth Avenue views. *700 Fifth Ave. (at 55th St.). www.peninsula.com.* ☎ *800/262-9467. 239 units. Double $490–$1,500, suite $1,375–$16,000. AE, DC, DISC, MC, V. Subway: E/F to Fifth Ave.*

★ **The Pod Hotel** MIDTOWN High style and high jinks at low rates—those are what travelers who stay here get. There's a trade-off of space (and, in some cases, a private bathroom) for groovy-looking if Lilliputian rooms—hence the word "pod." But the common areas are so fun-filled, with hopping bar/restaurants and ping-pong tables, that most don't mind. The Pod has a sister hotel with slightly higher rates at 39th Street. *230 E. 51st St., off Third Ave. www.thepodehotel. com.* ☎ *800/742-5945 or 212/355-0300. 348 units. $115–$190 double. AE, MC, V. Subway: 6 to 50th St.*

★ **The Roger** MURRAY HILL This under-the-radar boutique hotel on Madison Avenue manages to be

The lounge of the Sofitel.

both hip (in-the-know staff, iPod docking stations) and comfy (quilts on plump beds), with a buzzing mezzanine lounge. *131 Madison Ave. (at 31st St.). www.theroger newyork.com.* ☎ *888/448-7788. 193 units. Double $175–$535. AE, DC, DISC, MC, V. Subway: 6 to 28th St.*

★ **Sofitel New York** MIDTOWN WEST   Built in 2000, the 30-story

Money-Saving Tips on Lodging

New York has the most expensive lodgings in the Americas—a fact you'll comprehend when you try to book a hotel. To get the best price, consider these tips. **Schedule in the off season and at off times:** Hotels charge premium rates around the Christmas holidays, and prices climb sky-high during major events, such as the NYC Marathon in early November. During January and February rates are often halved; the same is true at Financial District hotels on weekends. **Look for outer borough and nearby New Jersey locations:** A number of big chains, such as Red Roof Inn and La Quinta, offer affordable offshoots in safe but less touristy Queens and Jersey City. Check out our reviews for the Nesva Hotel (p 161) and the Country Inn & Suites (p 158), both excellent options in Queens. **Check hotel websites** for exclusive online deals; you'll need to be members of the loyalty program to see the lowest rates, but joining is free. **Consider hotels where rooms share baths**—this one small inconvenience can save you big at hotels like downtown's **The Jane** (p 160), the **Larchmont** (p 160) and the **Pod Hotels** (p 163).

Sofitel has an elegant, marbled lobby with a Deco-style restaurant and bar. Rooms are standard but spacious and soundproofed. *45 W. 44th St. (btw. Fifth and Sixth aves.). www.sofitel.com.* ☎ *212/354-8844. 398 units. Double $219–$948. AE, DC, MC, V. Subway: B/D/F/M to 42nd St.*

★★ **The Surrey** UPPER EAST SIDE   An enviable Museum Mile location just adds to the allure of the Surrey, which melds its classic Art Deco roots with contemporary art. Rooms vary in size from spacious suites to standard, although well-equipped, rooms. What really sets the Surrey apart are the extras, such as a rooftop garden, a Cornelia spa, dreamy Duxiana mattresses, and room service from the acclaimed Café Boulud. *20 E. 76th St. (at Madison Ave.).* ☎ *212/288-3700. 189 units. Double $354–$762. AE, DC, DISC, MC, V. Subway: 6 to 77th St.*

The Wall Street Inn FINANCIAL DISTRICT   This intimate, seven-story Lower Manhattan oasis is warm, comforting, and very inexpensive on weekends. One warning though: the rooms that overlook rowdy Stone Street can get loud in warm weather because of all the outside bars. *9 S. William St. (at Broad St.). www.thewallstreetinn. com.* ☎ *212/747-1500. 46 units. Double $159–$399. AE, DC, DISC, MC, V. Subway: 2/3 to Wall St.; 4/5 to Bowling Green.*

★ **Washington Square Hotel** GREENWICH VILLAGE   Itsy bitsy rooms, but well-appointed and in a hotel with a storied history. Plus you're overlooking one of the loveliest parks in the city. *103 Waverly Place (btw. Fifth and Sixth aves.). www.wshotel.com.* ☎ *212/777-9515. 150 units. Double $215–$385. AE, MC, V. Subway: A/B/C/D/E/F/M to W. 4th St. (use 3rd St. exit).* ●

B&Bs & Apartment Stays

Yes, hotel prices are high in New York, and the costs climb even higher for families paying for extra people in the room. Oh, and did we mention hotel room taxes? (Tack on 14.25% to your total bill.) Save big bucks, enjoy more room, and live among the locals by staying in a B&B. Alas, apartment rentals of less than 30 days are now illegal, but many flout the law and find rooms through **AirBnB. com**, **HomeAway.com**, and **VRBO.com**. If that idea makes you nervous (and the city of NY announced in 2016 that it would be dedicating $10 million to shuttering "illegal hotels," i.e., rentals), know that you can stay legally in a room in an apartment so long as the owner is still in residence—and this can often yield BIG savings. You'll find such rooms through **Wimdu.com** and **Airbnb**.

The Savvy Traveler

Before You Go

The Best Times to Go

July and August are hot and humid, but because the local population tries to escape, the city is far less crowded. There are plenty of free alfresco events, too. December brings crowds and the highest hotel rates; January and February are the cheapest months to visit, by far, but very chilly. Ideal time? There's nothing like New York in late spring or fall when the weather is mild.

Festivals & Special Events

WINTER From a week or two before Thanksgiving through New Year's, the city puts on its Christmas decorations, highlighted by the **Rockefeller Center Christmas Tree** and displays at various department stores. On **New Year's Eve,** the most famous party of them all takes place in Times Square (www.timessquarenyc.org). During **Chinese New Year** (last week in January), Chinatown comes alive with parades and special celebrations (www.explorechinatown.com).

SPRING The **Pier Antiques Show,** the city's largest antiques show, takes place in March (www.pierantiquesshow.com) as does, of course, the **St. Patrick's Day Parade** (http://nycstpatricksparade.org) on the 17th. The **Easter Parade**—not a traditional parade, but a flamboyant fashion display along Fifth Avenue from 48th to 57th streets—is on Easter Sunday.

SUMMER All summer long, the **Lincoln Center Festival** (www.lincolncenterfestival.org; ☎ 212/7210-6500) celebrates the best of the performing arts from all over the world (tickets go on sale in late May). **SummerStage**

(www.summerstage.org; ☎ 212/360-2756) is a summer-long festival of outdoor performances in Central Park, featuring world music, pop, folk, and jazz artists. At the same time and also in Central Park, well-known actors take on the Bard in the Public Theater's long-running **Shakespeare in the Park** series (http://shakespeareinthepark.org). The **Independence Day Harbor Festival and Fourth of July Fireworks Spectacular** (☎ 212/484-1222, or Macy's Visitor Center at 212/494-4662) takes place on July 4. Dance till you drop at **Midsummer Night Swing** (http://new.lincolncenter.org/live; ☎ 212/875-5456), 3 weeks of outdoor dance parties held in Lincoln Center's Damrosch Park.

FALL The **West Indian–American Day Parade** (http://wiadca.com; ☎ 718/467-1797), an annual Brooklyn event on Labor Day, is New York's best street festival. The **Greenwich Village Halloween Parade** (www.halloween-nyc.com) on October 31 is a flamboyant parade that everyone is welcome to join. Two things everyone should see at least once are the **Radio City Music Hall Christmas Spectacular** (www.radiocitychristmas.com/newyork; ☎ 212/247-4777 or Ticketmaster at 212/307-1000) and the **Macy's Thanksgiving Day Parade** (☎ 212/494-4495).

Useful Websites

- **www.nycgo.com:** A wealth of free information about the city

- **www.nymag.com:** Terrific coverage of arts and events from *New York* magazine

- **www.timeout.com/newyork:** Full listings, restaurant reviews, shopping, and nightlife

- **www.panynj.gov** and **www.mta.info:** Transit info

- **www.weather.gov:** Up-to-the-minute weather

Restaurant & Theater Reservations

We can't say it enough: Book well in advance if you're determined to eat at a particular spot or see a very popular show (like *Hamilton*)—especially if you're visiting at a peak time. If you're determined to eat at a hot restaurant, ask for early or late hours—often tables are available before 6:30pm and after 9pm. Or ask about seating at the bar, which is often the best venue in the house anyway.

For advance theater bookings, try a discounter website like BroadwayBox.com first, as you may be able to get a less expensive seat that way. If that doesn't work, contact www.telecharge.com.

Getting **There**

By Plane

Three major airports serve New York City: **John F. Kennedy International Airport** in Queens is about 15 miles (24km; 1 hr. driving time) from midtown Manhattan; **LaGuardia Airport**, also in Queens, is about 8 miles (13km; 30 min.) from Midtown; and **Newark International Airport** (☎ 973/961-6000) in nearby New Jersey is about 16 miles (26km; 45 min.) from midtown. Always allow extra time, though, especially during rush hour, peak holiday travel times, and if you're taking a bus. Information on all three is available online at **www.panynj.gov/airports**.

For ease and convenience, your best bet is to stay away from public transportation when traveling to and from the airport. **Taxis** and **Uber** are a quick and convenient alternative. Taxis are available at designated taxi stands outside the terminals; all take credit cards. Fares, whether fixed or metered, do not include bridge and tunnel tolls ($8–$10) or a tip for the cabbie (15–20 percent is customary). They do include all passengers in the cab and luggage. Yellow cabs also charge a $1 surcharge weekdays from 4pm to 8pm and a 50¢ surcharge daily from 8pm to 6am. **From JFK:** Taxis charge a flat rate of $52 to Manhattan (plus tolls and tip). **From LaGuardia:** $24 to $30, metered, plus tolls and tip. **From Newark:** The dispatcher for New Jersey taxis gives you a slip of paper with a flat rate ranging from $50 to $75 (toll and tip extra), depending on where you're going in New York City. The yellow-cab fare from Manhattan to Newark is the meter amount plus $15 and tolls (about $69–$75, perhaps a few dollars more with tip).

Uber, Lyft and private limo companies provide convenient 24-hour door-to-door airport transfers. They usually are equal in cost to taxis. If you don't want to do Uber or Lyft on your phone when you arrive, you can get advance reservations for car services such as **Dial 7** (www.dial7.com; ☎ 800/777-7777) or **Carmel** (☎ 800/922-7635 or 212/666-6666).

AirTrains ($5–$14) are available at Newark and JFK and will certainly save you money, but skip the AirTrain JFK if you have mobility issues, mountains of luggage, or small children. You'll find it easier to rely on a taxi, car service, or shuttle service that can offer you door-to-door transfers. For information, check out **AirTrain JFK** (www.airtrainjfk.com) and **AirTrain Newark** (www.airtrainnewark.com; ☎ 888/EWR-INFO). The latter works pretty well, but you will have to change trains at a NJ Transit station to get to Penn Station in midtown Manhattan.

Bus and shuttle services provide a comfortable and less expensive (but usually more time-consuming) option than taxis and car services. The blue vans of **SuperShuttle** (www.supershuttle.com; ☎ 800/258-3826) serve all three airports; fares are $15 to $25 per airport. **The New York Airport Service** (www.nyairportservice.com; ☎ 718/560-3915) buses travel from JFK and LaGuardia to the Port Authority Bus Terminal (42nd St. and Eighth Ave.), Grand Central Terminal (Park Ave., btw. 41st & 42nd sts.), and to select midtown hotels. One-way fares run between $12 and $25 per person.

By Car

From New Jersey and points west, there are three Hudson River crossings into the city's west side: the **Holland Tunnel** (lower Manhattan), the **Lincoln Tunnel** (Midtown), and the **George Washington Bridge** (upper Manhattan). From upstate New York, the **Tappan Zee Bridge** spans the Hudson. For the east side, the **Brooklyn, Manhattan, Williamsburg,** and **Queensboro bridges,** as well as the **Queens Midtown Tunnel,** cross the East River from Brooklyn and Queens.

Once you arrive in Manhattan, park your car in a garage (expect to pay $35–$55 per day) and leave it there. You really don't need your car for traveling within the city (in fact, it can be more of a hindrance to drive it around the city, especially during rush hours).

By Train

Amtrak (www.amtrak.com; ☎ 800/USA-RAIL; book early—as much as 6 months in advance—and travel on weekends for best rates) runs frequent service to New York City's **Penn Station,** on Seventh Avenue between 31st and 33rd streets, as do **New Jersey Transit** and **Long Island Railroad. Metro-North Railroad** runs out of **Grand Central Terminal** (p 7). You can easily pick up a taxi, Uber, subway, or bus to your hotel from either station.

Getting **Around**

By Subway

The **subway** system is the fastest way to travel around New York, especially during rush hours. The subway runs 24 hours a day, 7 days a week. The rush-hour crushes are roughly from 8 to 9:30am and from 5 to 6:30pm on weekdays. The fare is $2.75 (half-price for seniors and those with disabilities); children under 44 inches tall (111cm) ride free. Fares are paid with a **MetroCard,** a magnetically encoded card that debits the fare when swiped through the turnstile (or the fare box on any city bus). MetroCards also allow you free transfers between the bus and subway within a 2-hour period. There are Pay-Per-Ride and Unlimited-Ride MetroCards; both can be purchased at any subway station.

By Bus

Less expensive than taxis, with hotter views than subway, buses would be the perfect alternative if they didn't sometimes get stuck in traffic. They're best for shorter distances or east to west journeys (in areas where the subways don't go crosstown). Like the subway fare, bus fare is $2.75, payable with a **MetroCard** or **exact change.** At some bus stops, you pay on the sidewalk; look for the kiosks. Bus drivers don't make change, and fare boxes don't accept dollar bills or pennies. If you pay with a Metro-Card, you can transfer to another bus or to the subway for free within 2 hours. If you pay cash, you must request a **free transfer** slip that allows you to change to an intersecting bus route only (legal transfer points are listed on the transfer paper) within 1 hour of issue. Transfer slips cannot be used to enter the subway.

By Taxi, Uber, Lyft, and Via

Yellow **taxi cabs** are licensed by the Taxi and Limousine Commission (TLC). Base fare on entering the cab is $2.50. The cost is 50¢ for every 1/5 mile or 50¢ per 1 minute in stopped or very slow moving traffic (or for waiting time); most take credit cards. There's no extra charge for each passenger or for luggage, but you must pay bridge or tunnel tolls. You'll also pay a 50¢ night surcharge after 8pm and before 6am, and a $1 peak-hour surcharge Monday to Friday 4 to 8pm. A 15 to 20% tip is customary. You can hail a taxi on any street.

As in other American cities, Uber, Lyft, and Via have become popular alternatives to taxis, and generally charge equivalent rates (with the exception of Via which is just $5 per person for rides of any distance). To use these services you'll need to download the apps to your smartphone.

By Bike

The **Citi Bike bike-sharing program** (www.citibikenyc.com; ☎ 855/245-3311) is a wonderful way to get around, especially now that the city has put special bike lanes onto many streets. Anyone over age 16 can purchase a 24-hour or weekly pass, which gives you access to any Citi Bike at 300-plus stations throughout the city for unlimited 30-minute trips (there are overtime fees if you don't dock a bike within 30 min.). Payment is made with a credit or debit card, and riders are given a code to enter on a keypad that unlocks the bike for use.

Fast **Facts**

ATMS (CASHPOINTS) You'll find **automated teller machines (ATMs)** every few blocks, all of which charge a fee to withdraw if you are not a customer of the bank (usually $3, not including any fees your home bank may charge).

BABYSITTING The first place to check is with your hotel. Many hotels have babysitting services or will provide you with lists of reliable sitters. If this doesn't pan out, call the **Babysitters' Guild** (www. babysittersguild.com; ☎ 212/682-0227). The sitters are licensed, insured, and bonded, and can even take your child on outings.

BANKING HOURS Banks tend to be open Monday through Friday from 9am to 6pm and Saturday mornings.

BUSINESS HOURS The city that never sleeps truly doesn't. Most stores stay open until 7pm or later, with drugstores and groceries usually going strong until 9pm, and delis and corner produce markets lasting into the wee hours. Most stores (except for in the Financial District) are open on Sunday, although they may not open until 11am or noon.

CONSULATES New York has a consulate for virtually every country. The consulate of **Australia** is at 150 E. 42nd St., 34th floor (☎ 212/351-6500). The consulate of **New Zealand** is at 222 E. 41st St., Ste. 2510 (www.nzembassy.com; ☎ 212/832-4038). The consulate of **Canada** is at 1251 Ave. of Americas (www.canadianembassy.org; ☎ 212/596-1628). The consulate of **Ireland** is at 345 Park Ave., 17th floor (www.irelandemb.org; ☎ 212/319-2555). The consulate of the **United Kingdom** is at 845 Third Ave. (www.britainusa.com; ☎ 212/745-0200).

DENTISTS If you have dental problems, a nationwide referral service known as **1-800-DENTIST** (☎ 800/336-8478) will provide the name of a nearby dentist or clinic.

DOCTORS The **NYU Downtown Hospital** offers physician referrals (☎ 888/698-3362).

ELECTRICITY Like Canada, the U.S. uses 110 to 120 volts AC (60 cycles), compared to 220 to 240 volts AC (50 cycles) in most of Europe, Australia, and New Zealand. If your small appliances use 220 to 240 volts, you'll need a 110-volt transformer and a plug adapter with two flat parallel pins to operate them here. Downward converters that change 220–240 volts to 110–120 volts are difficult to find in the U.S., so bring one with you.

EMERGENCIES Dial ☎ **911** for fire, police, and ambulance. If you encounter serious problems, contact **Traveler's Aid International** (www.travelersaid.org; ☎ 202/546-1127) to help direct you to a local branch. This nationwide, nonprofit, social-service organization geared to helping travelers in difficult straits offers services that might include reuniting families separated while traveling, providing food and/or shelter to people stranded without cash, or even offering emotional counseling.

GAY & LESBIAN TRAVELERS All over Manhattan, but especially in such neighborhoods as the **West Village, Hell's Kitchen, and Chelsea,** shops, services, and restaurants cater to a gay and lesbian clientele. It's unlikely you'll experience any forms of discrimination in New York City.

HOLIDAYS Banks, government offices, post offices, and many stores, restaurants, and museums are closed on the following legal national holidays: January 1 (New Year's Day), the third Monday in January (Martin Luther King, Jr., Day), the third Monday in February (Presidents' Day, Washington's Birthday), the last Monday in May (Memorial Day), July 4 (Independence Day), the first Monday in September (Labor Day), the second Monday in October (Columbus Day), November 11 (Veterans' Day), the fourth Thursday in November (Thanksgiving Day), and December 25 (Christmas). Also, the Tuesday following the first Monday in November is Election Day and is a federal government holiday in presidential-election years (held every 4 years, and next in 2020).

INSURANCE Trip-cancellation **insurance** helps you get your money back if you have to back out of a trip, if you have to go home early, or if your travel supplier goes bankrupt. To find the best policy for you, we recommend such marketplace sites as **SquareMouth. com** and **TravelInsurance.com**.

MAIL & POSTAGE The main post office is at 421 Eighth Ave. (at 33rd St.); other branches can be found by logging onto **www.usps.gov**. At press time, domestic postage rates were 33¢ for a postcard and 47¢ for a letter.

MONEY Most businesses and restaurants take plastic, and if they don't, there's an ATM or bank on just about every street corner. (Even cabs take credit cards.)

PHARMACIES Duane Reade (www. duanereade.com) has 24-hour pharmacies in **Midtown** at 250 W. 57th St., at Broadway (☎ 212/541-9708); on the **Upper West Side** at 2069 Broadway at 72nd Street (☎ 212/580-0497); and on the **Upper East Side** at 1279 Third Ave., at 74th Street (☎ 212/744-2668), as well as other locations. **CVS** (www.cvs.com) also has 24-hour pharmacies around the city.

SAFETY New York is one of the safest large cities in the U.S. But that doesn't mean you should take a stroll through Central Park in the wee hours of the morning, leave unsecured valuables in your car, or flash wads of cash in Times Square. No, no, and no. Avoid being the victim of petty crime by using common sense: Store your wallet in a safe place; wear your purse so it's not snatchable (although you don't have to wear your backpack on your front—that's just silly); lock up any valuables in the hotel safe; and avoid low trafficked areas especially at night.

SENIOR TRAVELERS New York subway and bus fares are half-price ($1) for people 65 and older. Many museums and sights (and some theaters and performance halls) offer discounted admission and tickets to seniors, so don't be shy about asking and always bring an ID card.

SMOKING Smoking is prohibited on public transportation, in hotel and office-building lobbies, in taxis, in bars and restaurants, and in all shops except cigar stores.

SPECTATOR SPORTS You've got your choice of baseball teams: the **Yankees** (www.yankees.com; ☎ 718/293-6000) or the **Mets** (www.mets.com; ☎ 718/507-TIXX). For basketball, there's the **Knicks** (www.nyknicks.com; ☎ 877/NYK-DUNK), the **New York Liberty** (www.wnba.com/liberty; ☎ 212/564-9622), and the **Brooklyn Nets** (www.nba.com/nets; ☎ 718/933-3000). The **New York Giants** (www.giants.com; ☎ 201/935-8222) and **Jets** (www.newyorkjets.com; ☎ 800/469-JETS) cover your football options. The **U.S. Open** takes place every August and is considered one of the premier events in tennis. For more info on that, go to www.usopen.org.

TAXES Sales tax is 8.875% on meals, most goods, and some services. **Hotel tax** is 14.75% plus $3.50 per room per night (including sales tax) **Parking garage tax** is 18.375% (residents get a reduced rate).

TELEPHONE For directory assistance, dial ☎ 411; for long-distance information, dial 1, then the appropriate area code and 555-1212. There are four area codes in the city: two in Manhattan, the original 212 and the newer 646, and two in the outer boroughs, the original 718 and the newer 347. The 917 area code is assigned to cellphones, pagers, and the like. Calls between these area codes are local, but you'll have to dial the area code plus the seven digits, even within your area code.

TICKETS Tickets for concerts at all larger theaters can be purchased through **Ticketmaster** (www.ticketmaster.com; ☎ 212/307-7171). For advance tickets at smaller venues, contact **Ticketweb** (www.ticketweb.com; ☎ 866/468-7619). You can buy theater tickets in advance from **TeleCharge** (www.telecharge.com; ☎ 212/239-6200) or **Ticketmaster** (www.ticketmaster.com; ☎ 212/307-4100). For sporting events and concerts, the reseller **Stubhub.com** can come in handy, especially for sold-out events. If you want last-minute tickets, see p 149.

TIPPING In hotels, tip **bellhops** at least $1 per bag ($2–$3 if you have a lot of luggage) and tip the **chamber staff** $1 to $2 per day (more if you've left a disaster area for him or her to clean up, or if you're traveling with messy kids and/or pets). Tip the **doorman** or **concierge** only if he or she has provided you with some specific service (such as calling a cab). In restaurants, bars, and nightclubs, tip **service staff** 15 to 20 percent of the check, tip **bartenders** 10 to 15 percent, and tip **checkroom attendants** $1 per garment. Tipping is not expected in cafeterias and fast-food restaurants. Tip **cab drivers** 15 to 20 percent of the fare and tip **skycaps** at airports at least $1 per bag ($2–$3 if you have a lot of luggage).

TOILETS Public restrooms are available at the city's main **visitor center** (1560 Broadway, btw. 46th and 47th sts. btw. 52nd and 53rd sts.). Grand Central Terminal, at 42nd Street between Park and Lexington avenues, and the High Line entrance at 16th Street and Tenth Avenue also have clean restrooms. Your best bet on the street is **Starbucks** or another city java chain—you can't walk more than a few blocks without seeing one. The big **chain bookstores** are good for this, too. On the Lower East Side, stop into the **Lower East Side Visitor Center,** 54 Orchard St., between Hester and Grand streets (Mon–Fri 9:30am–5:30pm, Sat–Sun 9:30am–4pm).

TOURIST OFFICES   NYC & Company is the city's official marketing and tourism organization, located at 810 Seventh Ave. (www.nycgo.com; ☎ 212/484-1200).

TOURS Scholar-led private or group walking tours with award-winning tour operator **Context Travel** (www.contexttravel.com; ☎ 800/691-6036) offer in-depth looks at the city's art, architecture, and urban history. Less expensive, but arguably as compelling are the walking tours given by **Free Tours by Foot** (www.freetoursbyfoot.com; you tip about $20 at the end). **Big Apple Greeter** (www.bigapplegreeter.org; ☎ 212/669-8159) provides free neighborhood walking tours given by locals (they're terrific and very personal). I'm not a fan of the hop-on, hop-off double-decker bus tours (they tend to be time wasters with poorly trained guides), but those offered by **Gray Line** (www.graylinenewyork.com; ☎ 800/669-0051) are the best of the bunch.

TRAVELERS WITH DISABILITIES   Public buses are an inexpensive and easy way to get around New York. All buses' back doors are supposed to be equipped with wheelchair lifts. Buses also "kneel," lowering their front steps for people who have difficulty boarding. Passengers with disabilities pay half-price fares ($1). The **subway** isn't yet fully wheelchair accessible, but a list of about 30 accessible subway stations and a guide to wheelchair-accessible subway itineraries are on the MTA website (**www.mta.nyc.ny.us/nyct**). All Broadway and most off-Broadway theaters have areas specially set aside for people in wheelchairs; call in advance to ask. You'll also find loaner wheelchairs and services for people with disabilities at such major touristic sites as the Metropolitan Museum and the 9/11 Memorial Museum.

A Brief **History of New York**

1524 Giovanni da Verrazano sails into New York Harbor.

1609 Henry Hudson sails up the Hudson River.

1621 The Dutch West India Company begins trading from New York City.

1626 The Dutch pay 60 guilders ($24) to the Lenape Tribe for the island of New Amsterdam.

1664 The Dutch surrender New Amsterdam to the British, and the island is renamed after the brother of King Charles II, the Duke of York.

1765 The Sons of Liberty burn the British governor in effigy.

1776 Independence from England is declared.

1789 The first Congress is held at Federal Hall on Wall Street, and George Washington is inaugurated.

1792 The first stock exchange is established on Wall Street.

1820 New York City is the nation's largest city, with a population of 124,000.

1863 Draft riots rage throughout New York; 125 people die, including 11 African Americans who are lynched by mobs of Irish immigrants.

1883 The Brooklyn Bridge opens.

1886 The Statue of Liberty is completed.

1892 Ellis Island opens and begins processing more than a million immigrants a year.

1904 The first subway departs from City Hall.

1920 Babe Ruth joins the New York Yankees.

1929 The stock market crashes.

1931 The Empire State Building opens and is the tallest building in the world.

1947 The Brooklyn Dodgers sign Jackie Robinson, the first African American to play in the Major Leagues.

1969 The Gay Rights movement begins with the Stonewall Rebellion in Greenwich Village. The Amazin' Mets win the World Series.

1990 David Dinkins is elected as the first African-American mayor of New York City.

2001 Terrorists use hijacked planes to crash into the Twin Towers of the World Trade Center, which brings both towers down and kills more than 3,000 people.

2003 Smoking is banned in all restaurants and bars.

2009 The New York Yankees win the World Series in their first year in the new Yankee Stadium, giving them 27 World Series championships.

2011 Same-sex marriage becomes legal in the state of New York.

2012 Hurricane Sandy, the worst storm to ever hit New York, bears down on the city and inflicts billions of dollars' worth of damage.

New York **Architecture**

New York is famous for its great buildings, but the truth is that the most interesting thing about its architecture is its diversity. From elegant Greek Revival row houses to soaring glass skyscrapers, the city contains examples of just about every style. Constructed over 300 years, these buildings represent the changing tastes of the city's residents from Colonial times to the present.

Georgian (1700–76)

This style reflects Renaissance ideas made popular in England, and later in the U.S., through the publication of books on 16th-century Italian architects. Georgian houses are characterized by a formal arrangement of parts employing a symmetrical composition enriched with classical details, such as columns and pediments.

St. Paul's Chapel (p 16), the only pre-Revolutionary building in Manhattan, is an almost perfect example of the Georgian style, with a pediment, colossal columns, Palladian window, quoins, and balustrade above the roofline.

Federal (1780–1820)

Federal was the first American architectural style. It was an adaptation of a contemporaneous English style called Adam (after Scottish architects Robert and James Adam), which included ornate, colorful interior decoration. Federal combined Georgian architecture with the delicacy of the French rococo and the classical architecture of Greece and Rome. The overall effect is one of restraint and dignity.

In the **West Village,** near and along Bedford Street between Christopher and Morton streets, are more original Federal-style houses than anywhere else in Manhattan. House nos. 4 through 10 (built 1834) on Grove Street, just off

Bedford, present one of the most authentic groups of late-Federal-style houses in America.

Greek Revival (1820–60)

The Greek Revolution in the 1820s, in which Greece won its independence from the Turks, recalled to American intellectuals the democracy of ancient Greece—and its elegant architecture. With many believing America to be the spiritual successor of Greece, the use of classical Greek forms came to dominate residential, commercial, and government architecture.

Perhaps the city's finest Greek Revival building is **Federal Hall National Memorial** (built 1842; p 58), 26 Wall St., at Nassau Street. The structure has a Greek temple

A typical Federal exterior.

front, with Doric columns and a simple pediment, resting on a high base called a plinth, with a steep flight of steps.

Gothic Revival (1830–60)

The term "Gothic Revival" refers to a literary and aesthetic movement of the 1830s and '40s in England and the U.S. that harked back to medievalism. Some structures had only one or two Gothic features, while others, usually churches, were copies of English Gothic structures.

Trinity Church (p 16), at Broadway and Wall Street (Richard Upjohn, 1846), is one of the most celebrated Gothic Revival structures in the U.S. Here you see all the features of a Gothic church: a steeple, battlements, pointed arches, Gothic tracery, stained-glass windows, flying buttresses (an external bracing system for supporting a roof or vault), and medieval sculptures.

Italianate (1840–80)

The architecture of Italy served as the inspiration for this building style, which could be as picturesque as the Gothic or as restrained as the classical. In New York, the style was used for urban row houses and commercial buildings. The development of cast iron at this time permitted the inexpensive mass production of decorative features that few could have afforded in carved stone. This led to the creation of cast-iron districts in nearly every American city.

New York's **SoHo Cast Iron Historic District** has 26 blocks jammed with cast-iron facades, many in the Italianate manner. The single richest section is **Greene Street** between Houston and Canal streets.

Early Skyscraper (1880–1920)

The invention of the skyscraper can be traced directly to the use of cast iron in the 1840s. Experimentation with cast and wrought iron in the construction of interior skeletons eventually allowed buildings to rise higher. These buildings were spacious, cost-effective, efficient, and quickly erected—in short, the perfect architectural solution for America's growing downtowns. But solving the technical problems of the skyscraper did not resolve how the buildings should look. Most solutions relied on historical precedents, including decoration reminiscent of the Gothic, Romanesque (characterized by rounded arches), or Beaux Arts.

Examples include the **American Surety Company,** at 100 Broadway (Bruce Price, 1895); the triangular **Flatiron Building** (p 34), at Fifth Avenue and 23rd Street (Daniel H. Burnham & Co., 1902), with strong tripartite divisions and Renaissance Revival detail; and the **Woolworth Building** (Cass Gilbert, 1913; p 18), on Broadway at Park Place.

Second Renaissance Revival (1890–1920)

Compared to the Italianate, or First Renaissance Revival (1840–90), this style showed a studied formalism, with greater faithfulness to Italian Renaissance precedents in its window and doorway treatments. It also differed in that it was used for larger-scale buildings, such as banks, swank town houses, government buildings, and private clubs.

New York's Upper East Side has two fine examples of this building type: the **Racquet and Tennis Club,** 370 Park Ave. (McKim, Mead & White, 1918), based on the style of an elegant Florentine palazzo; and the **Metropolitan Club,** 1 E. 60th St. (McKim, Mead & White, 1894).

Beaux Arts (1890–1920)

This style takes its name from the Ecole des Beaux-Arts in Paris, where a number of prominent American architects trained, beginning around the mid–19th century. These architects adopted the academic design principles of the Ecole, which emphasized the study of Greek and Roman structures, composition, and symmetry. Because of the idealized classical origins, the Beaux Arts in America was seen as the ideal style for expressing civic pride. Grandiose compositions, an exuberance of detail, and a variety of stone finishes typify most Beaux Arts structures.

The **New York Public Library** (p 39), at Fifth Avenue and 42nd Street (Carrère & Hastings, 1911), is perhaps the best example. Others of note are **Grand Central Terminal** (p 7), at 42nd Street and Park Avenue (Reed & Stem and Warren & Whetmore, 1913), and the **Alexander Hamilton U.S. Custom House** (Cass Gilbert, 1907), on Bowling Green between State and Whitehall streets.

International Style (1920–45)

In 1932, the Museum of Modern Art hosted its first architecture exhibit, titled simply *Modern Architecture*. Displays included images of International Style buildings from around the world. The structures all share a stark simplicity and vigorous functionalism, a definite break from historically based, decorative styles. The International Style was popularized in the U.S. through the teachings and designs of **Ludwig Mies van der Rohe** (1886–1969), a German émigré based in Chicago. Interpretations of the "Miesian" International Style were built in most U.S. cities as late as 1980.

Two famous examples of this style in New York are the **Seagram Building,** at 375 Park Ave. (Ludwig Mies van der Rohe, 1958), and the **Lever House,** at 390 Park Ave., between 53rd and 54th streets (Skidmore, Owings & Merrill, 1952).

Art Deco (1925–40)

Art Deco is a decorative style that took its name from a Paris exposition in 1925. The jazzy style embodied the idea of modernity, and it influenced all areas of design, from jewelry and household goods to cars, trains, and ocean liners. Art Deco buildings are characterized by a linear, hard edge, or angular composition, often with a vertical emphasis and highlighted with stylized decoration.

Despite the effects of the Depression, several major Art Deco structures were built in New York in the 1930s, often providing crucial jobs. **Rockefeller Center** (Raymond Hood, 1940; p 8) includes 30 Rockefeller Plaza, a tour de force of Art Deco style, with a soaring vertical shaft and aluminum details. The **Chrysler Building**'s needlelike spire (William van Alen, 1930; p 34), with zigzag patterns in glass and metal,

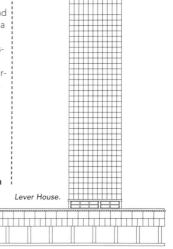

Lever House.

The Chrysler Building

Is a distinctive feature on the city's skyline. The **Empire State Building** (Shreve, Lamb & Harmon, 1931; p 7) contains a black- and silver-toned lobby among its many Art Deco features.

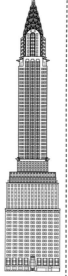

Art Moderne (1930–45)

Art Moderne strove for modernity and an artistic expression for the sleekness of the Machine Age. Unbroken horizontal lines and smooth curves visually distinguish it from Art Deco and give it a streamlined effect. It was popular with movie theaters and was often applied to cars, trains, and boats to suggest the idea of speed.

Radio City Music Hall (p 9), on Sixth Avenue at 50th Street (Edward Durrell Stone and Donald Deskey, 1932), has a sweeping Art Moderne marquee.

Postmodern (1975–90)

Postmodernism burst on the scene in the 1970s with the reintroduction of historical precedents in architecture. With many feeling that the office towers of the previous style were too cold, postmodernists began to incorporate classical details and recognizable forms into their designs– often applied in outrageous proportions.

The **Sony Building,** at 550 Madison Ave. (Philip Johnson/John Burgee, 1984), brings the distinctive shape of a Chippendale cabinet to the New York skyline.

Contemporary (1990–Today)

In just the last decade, such "Starchitectects" as Frank Gehry, Jean Nouvel, and others have added sinous, fractured, and asymmetrical buildings to the cityscape, in forms that couldn't have been achieved without the help of computer modeling. You'll see our picks for some of the best of these newbies on p 36.

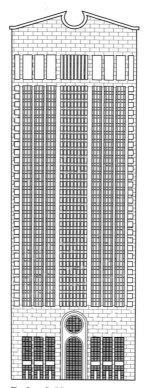

The Sony Building.

Index

See also Accommodations and Restaurant indexes, below.